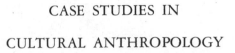

CASE STUDIES IN

CULTURAL ANTHROPOLOGY

GENERAL EDITORS
George and Louise Spindler
STANFORD UNIVERSITY

BECOMING A WOMAN IN RURAL BLACK CULTURE

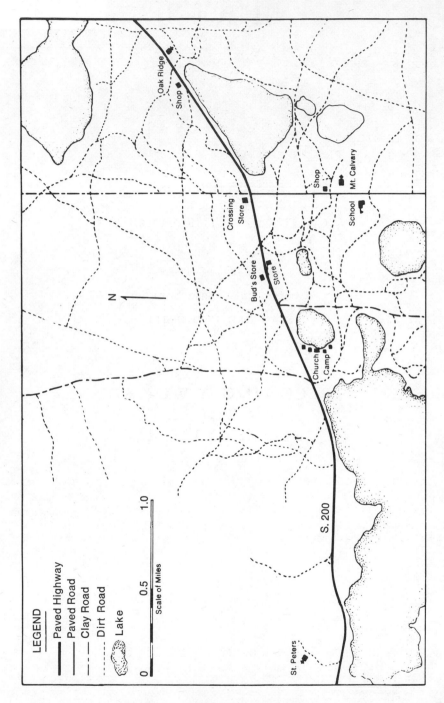

Figure 1. Map of Edge Crossing.

BECOMING A WOMAN
IN RURAL
BLACK CULTURE

By

MOLLY CROCKER DOUGHERTY

University of Florida, Gainesville

HOLT, RINEHART AND WINSTON

NEW YORK   CHICAGO   SAN FRANCISCO   ATLANTA

DALLAS   MONTREAL   TORONTO   LONDON   SYDNEY

Library of Congress Cataloging in Publication Data

Dougherty, Molly Crocker.
  Becoming a woman in rural Black culture.
  (Case studies in cultural anthropology)
  Bibliography: p. 109
  1. Afro-American women—Florida. 2. Afro-American
families—Florida. 3. Florida—Social conditions.
I. Title. II. Series.
E185.93.F5D68   301.41′2′0973   77-24218
ISBN 0-03-014921-5

Foreword

About the Series

These case studies in cultural anthropology are designed to bring to students, in beginning and intermediate courses in the social sciences, insights into the richness and complexity of human life as it is lived in different ways and in different places. They are written by men and women who have lived in the societies they write about and who are professionally trained as observers and interpreters of human behavior. The authors are also teachers, and in writing their books they have kept the students who will read them foremost in their minds. It is our belief that when an understanding of ways of life very different from one's own is gained, abstractions and generalizations about social structure, cultural values, subsistence techniques, and the other universal categories of human social behavior become meaningful.

About the Author

Molly Dougherty received a Bachelor's of Science in Nursing from the University of Florida in 1965 and was employed as a staff nurse in maternity units in three hospitals in the eastern United States. Her experience with women in childbirth from middle- and low-income backgrounds led her to examine the social and emotional meaning of birth and parenthood for women and their families in various segments of this society. Interests relating to pregnancy and parenting led her to a Master's in Nursing in 1968 and to a doctorate in Anthropology at the University of Florida in 1973. She is an Associate Professor of Nursing at the University of Florida, where she teaches graduate students in Maternal, Infant, and Women's Health. She holds an appointment in the Department of Anthropology.

Molly has had long exposure to rural life and resides in an area not unlike Edge Crossing, discussed in this case study. She lives with her husband, Ed Dougherty, and their two young daughters, Ann and Lynn. She and her family enjoy outdoor activities and are interested in raising livestock, gardening, and camping.

Professional interests of the author include health of minorities, health behaviors in community settings, women's health, and population. She is involved with the Gainesville Women's Health Center, which is directed and controlled by women. Its mission is to return the control of health services to health-care recipients and to provide participatory well-women gynecologic services.

About the Book

This case study has several very important assets. It is a study of a southern black community, and studies of southern black communities have been notably absent since the 1930s. It is a study written by a young woman about the community and life-cycle passages within it from the viewpoint of the women. It is organized with a strong conceptual framework utilizing workable, modern theoretical constructs. It also happens that this study is written in such a manner that most readers will enjoy it, though the material on which it is based is subjected to a disciplined analysis.

Part One focuses on the community (Edge Crossing), describing the use of space, including natural features, households and yards, and gathering places; the rhythm of social activities as ordered by time and space and the separation of sex roles; the rites of intensification such as ball games and religious services; and encounters with economic and educational systems external to the core of community meaning and resource allocation. Part Two discusses kinship and family organization over generational time and illustrates the flexibility of the system, the sharing of maternal roles and child care among related women, and interpersonal relationships of children with one another and with adults. Parts One and Two prepare the way for the detailed analysis of female adolescent maturation in Part Three. The author analyzes adolescence following the schema of rites of passage, emphasizing courtship and the drama of childbirth. The analytic framework is supplied by skillful utilization of concepts from both Van Gennep and Victor Turner.

Readers will find this case study and *Lifelines: Black Families in Chicago* (this series), by Joyce Aschenbrenner, complementary to each other. Though Dougherty has reported on a small rural community in the South and Aschenbrenner on a segment of a great urban aggregate in the North, there are some clear continuities, centering particularly on sex roles, courtship, and on familiar and extended kin relations and obligations. Black culture in the United States assumes a very different texture and shape in these studies than in those produced during the time, only a few years back, when black social life was interpreted by social scientists as essentially a form of social disorganization. The differences between white middle class and black culture also emerge, along with the recognition of an organized but flexible black way of life.

This case study by Professor Dougherty is a notable contribution to the growing list of case studies in this series, and elsewhere, written by anthropologists who have turned to the study of segments of our own complex, many-faceted society.*

GEORGE AND LOUISE SPINDLER
General Editors

San Diego, Spain

* See list of Case Studies in Contemporary American Culture at the end of this book.

Acknowledgments

The persons contributing to the ideas and information in this manuscript are too numerous to mention. Although a formal expression of gratitude does not diminish my indebtedness, I would like to thank them here.

The faculty of the Department of Anthropology at the University of Florida have been influential in my education in anthropology and have each contributed uniquely to my understanding of human behavior. Professor G. Alexander Moore, chairman of my Graduate Advisory Committee, has patiently and diplomatically guided me through the rigors of authorship and the final months of field research. His ideas, transmitted to me in graduate seminars over two years, are reflected here and will remain a part of my orientation to social anthropology. Ella Lawson, James Payne, and Lucille Wilson each read the manuscript and offered valuable comments; their assistance is appreciated, but only the author is responsible for the contents herein.

The use of census material depended upon the help of J. Ray Jones, Research Librarian, who led me in the acquisition of census material, and Paul L. Doughty, chairman of the Department of Anthropology, who secured computer time for my use. The patient and accurate typing was provided by Barbara Coaxum.

The funding agencies making graduate study and research economically feasible are also to be mentioned. I was supported during the years 1969–1973 by Department of H.E.W. Special Nurse Fellowship numbers 1F04-NU-27, 257-01, 5F04-NU-27,257-02, 5F04-NU-27,257-03, 4F04-NU-27,257-04, 2F04-NU-27,257-05, and 4F04-NU-27,257-06. The research was also supported by a research award from Alpha Theta Chapter of Sigma Theta Tau, National Honor Society of Nursing, and a research grant from the Research Committee of National Sigma Theta Tau. Without these sources of research funding the field work would have been much more difficult.

Ed Dougherty has provided reassurance and support in innumerable ways. All photographs and figures are his creations. To him I owe great thanks.

Gratitude to my informants cannot be expressed by touching pen to paper. Through works and actions I hope I have and will continue to demonstrate my appreciation to them.

M.C.D.

Contents

BECOMING A WOMAN
IN RURAL
BLACK CULTURE

Introduction

This study describes the way girls develop into women in a rural black community in north central Florida which I have called Edge Crossing. Becoming a woman in any community involves acquiring certain emotions, attitudes, beliefs, and behaviors similar to those displayed by other female adults. Womanhood suggests adult bonding, sexual relationships, and motherhood. Certain sequences of maturational events and the development of attitudes, beliefs, and resultant behaviors distinguish the path toward womanhood in Edge Crossing. The social realities of the kinship system, courtship patterns, and maternal behavior are crucial factors in the process. To understand these, the social organization of the community and the external forces shaping that community must be studied. These are described to the reader in this case study.

BACKGROUND READING

Although New World blacks have been the subject of research for many years, the available literature contributes little to the understanding of female social maturation. Social patterns of New World and United States black populations are often analyzed as adaptations to marginality and as a response to limited access to the resources of wider society. New World black studies were first stimulated by Herskovits (1930, 1941), who sought New World social forms having African counterparts.

Research among black populations in the United States has been influenced by the sociological tradition and the contributions of Frazier (1932, 1939, 1949) and Herskovitz (1941). Community studies conducted in the South in the 1930s (Dollard 1937; Davis and Dollard 1940; Davis et al. 1941) focused on the prevailing caste system and its effect on social life. Powdermaker (1939) and Johnson (1934, 1941) present southern black women as highly reproductive, influential in the family, and intensely involved in the child-rearing process. Although Lewis (1955) carried out a community study among blacks in a North Carolina town, there was little other research among blacks in the 1940s and 1950s. Models of black community and domestic organization which may apply to the United States situation have been presented by Smith (1956), Gonzalez (1965, 1969), and others. The central position of the female in the domestic organization is thought to be related to the restrictions on black male participation in the economic and political institutions of the wider society throughout the Western hemisphere.

Blacks in the urban North became the focus of research interest in the 1960s. These studies interpreted black social organization as a disorganized or deviant form of white models (Rainwater and Yancey 1967; Glazer and Moynihan 1963; Billingsley 1968). These findings are related to Frazier's (1932) assertion that the slave heritage destroyed the family and kinship structure. However, this disorganization model was countered by anthropological research seeking the internal organization of the system through empirical, comparative research. Liebow (1967) and Hannerz (1969, 1970) describe male behavior and its relationship to the internal organization of the urban black community and the white-dominated political and economic superstructure. In urban research, recurrent themes are lack of access to the resources of wider society (Hannerz 1970) and poverty (Abrahams 1964, 1970; Kochman 1970; Lomax 1970; Haralambos 1970). Differing interests and activities of males and females, individualism, and egalitarianism are described as forms of black experience. Stack (1974), who studied an urban black community in the Midwest, analyzes the social networks and reciprocities of community members. The parenting roles and male-female relationships described by Stack have similarities to those described in this study. Another recent study (Aschenbrenner 1975) describes kinship among black families in Chicago who maintain relationships with relatives in the South. The parallels between this research and Aschenbrenner's findings are striking. Individuals who leave Edge Crossing for the North could easily become established in kin-based groups like those Aschenbrenner describes.

Although Young (1970) discusses divergent themes in the literature, field observations of children, and unique interaction patterns in a small southern town, research among southern black populations has been neglected since the 1930s. Yet blacks in the rural South and urban North are linked by a common cultural tradition. Many of the distinctive social forms observed in the urban situation are also identifiable in Edge Crossing. The separation of male-female roles, the character of male social interactions beyond the home, and the emotional release in religion and entertainment described in this case study are of interest in the study of the whole of black culture, and contribute to our understanding of cultural continuity and change.

The study of women and the attempt to define their particular social behavior and role is a recent interest in the social sciences. Most research has emphasized public or male-dominated behavior and, therefore, has resulted in few careful descriptions of female social behavior or of the transitional phases in the female life cycle relating to her reproductive capacity. Women are traditionally described in terms of their contribution to the domestic domain and the reproduction and socialization of children. Females in Edge Crossing conform to the traditional image of women in that domesticity and motherhood are central to the female role. Yet there are significant departures from traditional behaviors because these females enjoy their sexuality, seek out sexual contacts, and are highly independent in the selection of partners. Females initiate action with males, behave as if courtship is a highly complex and competitive game, and bring forth children to validate courtship bonds. Although they have limited access to the educational, economic, occupational, and political resources of society, they carry significant economic and social responsibility. They are permitted considerable freedom in the selection of partners and independence in seeking economic resources. The female role in

Edge Crossing is a complex combination of public and private behavior which is learned from other women and through associations with men. Research upon which this case study is based examines the process by which girls become women and learn the feminine role in their social milieu.

THE FIELD RESEARCH

This research, carried out between November 1971 and December 1972, resulted from an interest in the biological regularities of, and social behavior surrounding, childbearing. Observations of black and white women during childbirth and the perception that their expectations and social supports differ were a part of my experience as a maternity nurse. My objective was to discover the beliefs, practices, and social supports that women experience during typical female life crises. Because there is little published about the social aspects of childbearing, black females, or southern blacks as a subcultural group, there were few models available around which to organize my thoughts. The situation seemed to be ideal for an exploratory, modified community study to produce formulations about female behavior.

Preparing for the field research led to my reading several volumes available in the popular press about blacks and by blacks (Jones 1961; Malcom X 1964; Brown 1965; Carmichael and Hamilton 1967; Cleaver 1968; Wright 1940; Grier and Cobbs 1968). The latent and overt hostility blacks are reported to have toward all whites frightened me. I thought that I might represent all the ills of white society to the people in the community.

After I had selected a community for study,[1] a white public health nurse offered to take me to a clinic there. I accepted, hoping to find a point of entry. I wanted to disassociate myself with agencies outside the community so that I would be seen as relatively independent of official agencies, making my own mistakes. The public health clinic was held at the school building, and I immediately noticed the Headstart class and met the teachers (both black) who utilized volunteers in their work. Although Headstart involvement did not lead me directly to the students' mothers as I had originally hoped, it was helpful in other ways. I learned the classroom routines, the children's names, and to understand the language; I also met some older women in the community. The Headstart cook was a generous woman with many visitors. When the students napped, I went to the kitchen and talked with her, or listened when she had visitors.

I did not, at first, go to homes in an attempt to meet people because that is the typical approach of white outsiders, bill collectors, and other nuisances. I bided my time and met people through the school, the senior citizens' organization, and the church. The process was very slow. I had to meet people, talk to them long enough to let them know my purpose in the community, and ask them if they would help me. Then I would ask if we could meet again and await an invitation to their homes. If they were willing to participate they would usually tell me how to get to their houses, or I would give them a ride home.

I told everyone that the information I gathered from them, and in the com-

---

[1] The presence of a lay midwife was the most important single criterion for selection.

munity, was going to be used in a paper I was writing, and that whatever they said would not be repeated to others in the community. They knew from the start that they were not going to tell me anything that was a secret, or as they said, would do anyone any "harm." My writing about what I learned seemed to confuse them because they did not see anything in their lives or in the community that was worth writing or reading about.

I realized that differences in the way we spoke English probably impeded their understanding of what I meant. I repeated my purpose, asked if they would participate, and repeatedly explained that I did not want them to feel obligated to help me if they were not sure about it. It was easier to transpose the concepts of research purpose, confidentiality, and writing into understandable forms after I knew their language patterns.

I found older women easier to meet, more willing to participate, at home more often, and more knowledgeable about the community, its history, and female behavior. In retrospect, I realize that forming contacts with older women was fortuitous because they function as guardians of information. When they felt I was acceptable, younger women became more open and available. Keeping names linked to faces, and understanding the relationships between persons and households was difficult, but alleviated somewhat by the collection of genealogical material. Genealogies were elicited from older women first, and then younger ones, adding to my knowledge about family, community, household relationships, personal names, and generational distinctions among kin.

During the first four months of the research my sensitivity to being out of place resulted in midday headaches and a desire to flee from anxiety-provoking situations. I also noticed that people talked much more slowly than I did, and were very indirect. I found that asking about institutional arrangements, religion, school, historical events, and genealogical material produced more information than did asking about living persons and current events. Eventually I got to know various persons, understood the language with ease, learned to be comfortable with silence, and could relate to our commonalities (child care, home, cooking, gardening, etc.).

I never met everyone who lives in the community. Males were among those with whom I had only limited contact. I assumed that involvement with males might raise questions about my purpose in the community since I was doing female-oriented research.

Men and women in Edge Crossing assume that male-female relationships have sexual overtones. Several of my informants related to me instances of males who had approached them to "talk to" me for them. The informants responded that I was married and had children, and that it was no use to "bother" with me. When they related the instances to me we laughed and joked about "how men be."

Although I had few associations with males, my approach to each person in the community was open friendliness. I am sure that I was sometimes kidded (jived) or misled, but I feel that the behavioral patterns and planning strategies became clear during the period of research.

One of the most rewarding relationships I had was with the lay midwife in the community. We became very friendly even though she was 45 years older than I. We taped hours of our discussions and her ideas. Eventually she and I traveled around visiting old friends and former clients of hers, which gave me insight into the networks that bind communities together. The information she gave me was used as a basis for gathering data from other informants. When I talked with others I covered similar topics with all of them.

Reciprocity in goods, services, and experiences seemed to validate the relationships that formed. Although there was not a direct relationship between the giving and receiving, it did tend to enhance the bonds I formed with others. I felt and tried to express that they were giving me (through their help) much more than I could ever return. However, reciprocity seemed to place the relationships on a personal basis, more comfortable for them and, eventually, for me.

The sharing of personal experiences was one direction that relationships took. Younger women revealed their personal lives to me and asked me questions about myself and white women in general. I revealed my personal and sexual behavior and my knowledge of white women and men to them more freely than I ordinarily do among other friends.

Goods also transferred hands on a regular, but unscheduled basis. I had a collard-green patch that produced prolifically and I took sacks filled with greens to informants who did not have greens in their gardens. Often fish and peas were saved for me. In addition, the use of my car proved to be a valuable asset in establishing relationships and in providing services to them. Frequently, once a week or more, I took between three and ten women and children into one of the towns to "trade" or attend to other business. On one occasion I had three adult women, eight children, seven bags of groceries, an overstuffed chair, a coffee table, and four pillows in my VW Squareback on the way back from town. In June, I took a group of high school students to the beach. There were seven people in the car as well as the food and paraphernalia they took along. These two examples stand out as exaggerated cases of the kinds of activities involved in the field work.

In the course of the research I went wherever informants' business took us. The traveling gave us time to talk and allowed me to witness their interactional patterns with various social agencies. The activities were varied; on different occasions I was at the jail, public health departments, clinics, the university, the community college, and innumerable places of business and entertainment in the towns and communities within 100 miles of Edge Crossing. The car was one of my most valuable research tools; I drove about 24,000 miles during the field work.

In addition to long-distance travel, the car was useful for getting to the scattered homes in the community. I visited and talked with informants daily or weekly, depending on the situation. I rarely stayed in a home less than 15 minutes, even if I was just dropping off a package or delivering a message. The longest I ever stayed in one home in a 24-hour period was 19 hours. Most of my contacts were between 1 and 3 hours. Early in the field work I had to force myself to stay in a home for a half hour; toward the end of the research I had to force myself to leave in an hour and a half so that I could meet with everyone I planned to see on a particular day.

The fact that I have two children gave me a basis of communication with women who relate easily to the problems and pleasures of motherhood. During the research I fell into a pattern that worked out satisfactorily. I spent the day in Edge Crossing and wrote up my field notes in the evening after the children were asleep. When I remained in the community into the evening or returned in the evening or on the weekend, my husband took care of the children. Informants knew that I was married and had children and seemed to understand my desire to be at home during part of the day. They were puzzled that my husband permitted me so much freedom and asked me whether he knew what I did. They seemed impressed that he stayed with our children; most fathers they know are not willing to baby-sit while women visit or go out. It took some time for people I did not know well to identify my role. They thought I was a teacher, a social worker, or employed on one of the OEO (Office of Economic Opportunity) projects.

The schedule I kept left little time for frivolity except with informant friends. I enjoyed the relaxing, joking, traveling, gossiping, and child care that occupied their time. The drive to and from Edge Crossing was time-consuming but I usually taped field notes while driving home. Throughout the research I needed time to reflect on my feelings about myself, informants, and events that occurred and to plan for future inquiry. I was able to do this while driving.

Exit from the field was more easily accomplished because informants thought of me as a person with an identity in the community, but also beyond it. I usually saw informants in their homes and some of them visited my home. My having a role apart from the community helped restrict the dependency relationships that developed. I am still in the community irregularly to attend church services and to visit friends. I maintain almost daily contact with one girl and another woman calls me when she needs transportation or other assistance. I expect that my contacts in the community will be maintained as long as I live in this area. Some informants became friends; they were distinct from me in various ways, but my personal involvement with them was more than a professional relationship. Unfortunately, the personal bonds that developed—the humor, the laughable miscommunications and friendships the women and I shared—are not a focus of this study.

DEMOGRAPHIC PROFILE

Demographic information is important for comparison with other studies. The demographic profile of the community includes the economic, educational, occupational, and population features of the area.

The north central Florida community of Edge Crossing is approximately 25 miles west of County Seat, a manufacturing and farming town with a population in 1970 of about 10,000. It is equidistant from University Town, an educational and medical center with a population of approximately 70,000 in 1970. In contrast to the state as a whole, the population of the county remained relatively stable between 1960 and 1974 (Flordia 1970:1; Thompson 1975:16). Over one-fourth of the population is nonwhite and about three-quarters of the population lives in rural areas.

The nonwhite population is characterized by low incomes, unskilled occupations, and low levels of education. The population is moderately young; over 50 percent of all persons are under 25 years of age while about 34 percent of them are under 15 years of age (Thompson 1975:16). The high proportion of adolescents in the area is due to the relatively high birth rate and the movement of adults out of the area for economic reasons.

Although marriage and childbearing tend to hamper educational efforts, females complete more years of education than males (U.S. Census 1970: Count Four). The higher educational levels of females relates to the occupational structure but is not directly reflected in individual incomes. Women in this area receive lower average incomes than males, a similarity they share with women throughout the nation. Yet females predominate in public-school teaching, the most common professional occupation in the area. Nearly all other persons are in semiskilled or unskilled occupations (U.S. Census 1970: Count Four), which is reflected in the low remuneration received by most of the black population. More than twice as many females as males have no income, illustrating the economic responsibility men bear. Nearly half the family incomes are under $3000 per year while an additional one-quarter have incomes under $6000 per year (U.S. Census 1970: Count Four).

In contrast, statistics for the white population indicate that whites in the same area experience higher incomes, occupational positions, and educational levels. The black population of the area is typified by low incomes, which is thought to affect other areas of social relations and health. Although a direct relationship has not been proven, it is known that low incomes and educational levels are often found among populations with high infant death rates, high birth rates, and other features relating to reproductive and child health.

Nonwhite women become pregnant more often and deliver more live infants, but they also experience still births and infant deaths more frequently than whites. The 1974 statistics for the county reveal that birth rates for whites and nonwhites were 13.0 and 21.5 respectively, while the infant mortality rate for whites was 11.9 and for nonwhites, 46.7 (Florida 1974: 26,98). Pregnancy occurs earlier in the reproductive years and birth rates for black women under 19 years of age are increasing (Florida 1970:14, 1974:34). In addition, over 50 percent of nonwhite births are to unmarried women; among whites about 7 percent are unmarried (Florida 1974:35). Although marital status of the mother is cited nationally as a significant factor in child health, in this community it appears to reflect distinctive black courtship and marriage patterns (discussed in Part Three).

At the time this research was planned and conducted (1970–1972) young women were delivering an increasing proportion of all births despite the greater availability of and knowledge about contraception. The trend toward younger women bearing a greater proportion of all births evident in this county is also true of the nation as a whole. Although it is convenient to assume that changing sexual patterns account for the change, alternative explanations are probably more telling. Mature women using more effective contraceptives, the trend toward having fewer children, and possibly better nutrition and other factors contributing to greater fecundity among adolescents are also explanations of this phenomenon.

PLAN OF THIS CASE STUDY

The conceptual framework has three major themes. First, *community* is described as a system of stable institutions and as the expression of fellowship among social equals. Second, the *kinship system* guides generational time and social maturation. Third, *rites of passage* are seen in adolescence with subphases in pregnancy, childbirth and acceptance of the mothering role. Girls become women by experiencing courtship, pregnancy, childbirth and mothering.

Use of space, economics, education, and ritual expression reflect customary social forms in Edge Crossing. The use of space is organized first by natural features, including lakes, woods, and buildings, but space is also organized to reflect social patterns. Households, where personnel fulfill biological and social needs, stores, serving economic and social functions, and shops, where both sexes meet and mingle, are spatially discrete entities. The use of space gives expression to the segregation of typically male and female behavior and their necessary interdependence produced by the division of labor.

Just as males share female-oriented space and households, males reserve for females positions in their social space. Stores and shops dominated by male activities are a forum for male-female interaction where females behave in socially defined ways toward males. Domestic space and household operations are female oriented. The distribution of males' economic resources to females in various households reserves for them an esteemed position in female-oriented space.

Space and time define locations and rhythms for social activities. The rhythms in homes, at work or school, and at group events occur in daily, weekly, monthly, and annual cycles and each occurs in a spatially circumscribed place. The temporal rhythms of work or school are punctuated by rites of intensification restoring equilibrium, expressing community unity, reestablishing the division of labor, and symbolically drawing residents together.

Rites of intensification occur on a weekly cycle, at ball games and most inclusively at church services. Religious rites, spatially separated from customary male and female-oriented space, bring both sexes and three generations together. The participation of all categories of personnel helps to intensify bonds, resolve conflicts, and restore equilibrium.

The kinship system provides another dimension of identification in the community. Kinship is analyzed through generational time to establish the patterns associated with inheritance and property. Kinship and descent described within a contemporary household reveal the movement of, and relationships among, personnel as maturation and adulthood are attained. The maturation of young women is described within the context of the community and the kinship system. Young women develop identification with family and kin and then establish roles in the community. They ultimately establish their independence and identity as members of each.

PART ONE   The Community

A social vignette sets the scene.

Twenty youths between 12 and 18 years of age step from the school bus returning them to Edge Crossing from junior and senior high school about 9 miles away. Chatting, they walk singly or in small groups in an irregular pattern as they fan out in various directions toward their own or friends' homes. Some carry purses or books while others are empty-handed; most are fashionably dressed. Among girls sizzle suits (very short, bare-backed dresses with matching bikini panties) are popular. The boys wear brightly colored pants and shirts and floppy knit or felt hats. One girl wears a loose fitting man's shirt; on the back is an inked-on clenched fist with "Black Power" printed below it. Most of the youths have Afro hair styles, although some of the girls wear their hair straightened. A few of the boys have their hair plaited down in a style popular since longer hair came into fashion.

Jean,[1] 16 years of age, steps off the bus wearing a short skirt and a man's shirt, bobby socks, and loafers. Unlike the others, she walks down the sidewalk of the old school building and into the cafeteria where Headstart pupils eat their meals. To the cook, her aunt, she says "Hey." Then turning to two little girls one and three years of age, she watches momentarily and then speaks softly, "Hey, Tina. How you doing, Joan?" She says nothing more to her aunt, focusing her attention on the little girls. After about three minutes she picks up a diaper bag, takes the younger child by the hand, and commands the older one, "Come on." They start down the path toward home about 400 yards away.

Jean takes care of the children until her parents return from work about midnight. Ordinarily, her grandmother, who lives further up the path, helps her, but today her grandmother is away at a funeral. Jean is to attend school during the day and take care of her youngest sister and her little daughter after school for two more years because her parents want her to finish high school. It is her responsibility to take care of the girls while her parents are away because her grandmother is old and her siblings do not come home on a regular schedule.

Jean and her ancestors have lived in Edge Crossing for five generations. It is

---

[1] All personal and place names are changed.

not mentioned on most maps of the area, but is a distinct place with stores, churches, homes, shops,[2] a playground, and numerous lakes. The school there was closed when county schools integrated in 1967–1968. Jean is involved in and affected by most of the activities in the community. She maintains relationships with her kin, her friends, the father of her daughter, and his friends and family. As a mother, young woman, student, church member, and daughter she has an identifiable role in the community.

Young women, similar in age and status to Jean, form a distinguishable social grouping and are present in most social settings, including church, school, home, and gathering places beyond the home. Their roles lack definition and authority although they are responsible individuals and family members. The process by which girls traverse the years between childhood and adulthood and the social changes they experience are examined here. To analyze the social behavior of girls it is necessary to understand the organization of the community in which they live and the social realities they face in becoming women. Although the purpose of the presentation is to elucidate the maturation of adolescent females, the description of the community provides a necessary foundation for the analysis. In Part One customary social forms, economic, and educational characteristics of the community are described; the use of space and its social meaning is discussed in Chapter 1.

---

[2] Businesses providing a focus for evening social interactions are called "shops" by local residents.

1 / Use of space

Community organization and customary social forms have spatial correlates in geography, settlement pattern, and housing in a community. The analysis of space use clarifies the social behavior in houses, yards, and gathering places beyond the home and permits the explication of the repetitive behavioral patterns organized around periodic temporal rhythms. The community is described first in terms of geography and settlement pattern involving the broad use of space in the community. Next, houses, yards, and the schedules of sleep, work, and recreation are related to domestic space and typical female behavior. Finally, male social behavior in stores and shops explicates the division between male and female domain, a recurrent theme throughout the presentation. Although male and female roles are segregated in socially and spatially recognized ways, they are related to one another in other ways. It is necessary to analyze various dimensions of the community to realize the interrelationships. We begin with a description of the geography and settlement pattern.

The residents of Edge Crossing live in clusters of houses scattered over a loosely defined area of about four square miles. The center of the community is the Crossing store (see Figure 1, frontispiece); the boundaries of the community become less well defined as households further from the store are considered.[1] Numerous lakes limit the use of space and add interest to the sandy land and scrub vegetation in the area. There are two paved roads in the community; one is a state-maintained highway (S-200) dividing the community. The other, intersecting with S-200, is paved south of the highway but clay to the north. There are two county-maintained clay roads running perpendicular to S-200 and innumerable sandy lanes cutting through woods and terminating in yards. Existing buildings, roads, and lakes structure the use of space while land possession determines who may live or work on specific properties.

Land ownership has always been important and older persons describe the transfer of land to present families from the original settlers who came into the area shortly after the Civil War. Some of the early settlers homesteaded as much as 100 acres of land, while others laid claim to considerably less. Some of the lands are held relatively intact while others have been divided numerous times after the deaths of local land holders. Some of the land around a lake south of Edge Crossing has been sold to whites, but for the most part, land has not transferred between blacks and whites.

Residents refer to numerous places in the community and beyond it by

[1] The area shown on the map (Figure 1) includes the area where most informants live.

name. For example, Bull Lake, Mining, and Greenville are all within the area defined as Edge Crossing. Then, beyond Edge Crossing are other places, equally rural, also called by name. Any person's or family's house within five or ten miles of the Crossing store can be located by place name, family name, or geographical description. A household or family can be located in space because they are near one lake or another, near a particular road or bend in the road, on a specific clay road, near a relative's home place, or near a store or church.

There has been a gradual increase in the population of the community. Older residents say that people live everywhere now; when they were young there were "woods everywhere." A definite movement of homes and persons toward S-200 has taken place and a tendency to build homes near the lakes and along county-maintained roads is noticeable. One of the attractions for moving nearer good roads has been the potential for mingling with others.

All gathering places are located on the two paved roads. The three stores, two shops, three churches, and the old school building are within two miles of one another. The events which occur at schools and churches are explored in later sections. The rhythm of activity at the stores, shops, and homes provides insight into the social use of space in the community.

HOUSES AND YARDS

The house and yard provide a focus for numerous individual and group activities including eating, resting, sleeping, care of clothing and bodily needs, child care, and the exchange of money and information between members of the household. Life in the home is usually shared with persons related by blood or marriage and includes persons from two or more generations.

Houses vary considerably in age, design, and location, reflecting the adaptations in construction through decades of time. A combination of house types are often located near one another so that the households function almost as one unit. These arrangements are created by two or more houses located within 50 feet of one another or by a mobile home being blocked up within 10 feet of an established house. Mobile homes permit greater flexibility in household arrangements than do houses because they can be located to meet the needs of related families and moved when needs change.

Housing located in close proximity and possessed by related families permits the households to function cooperatively. Cooking, child care, laundry, and sleeping arrangements alternate between the households.

Clustered houses, cooperating in various ways, are usually owned by related persons who obtained a portion of the family land on which to build a home from older relatives. In some cases, transfer of land title occurs, but the adult sons and daughters are usually permitted to use family land until the death of the parents, when the land becomes part of their inheritance. The housing patterns and the way they are grouped over the land is related to land possession and tenure, discussed in Chapters 5 and 6.

Housing in the community reflects the adaptation to construction methods developed over the years, but the spatial orientation of housing indicates the importance of kinship and land possession. The interiors of the homes are adorned with the artifacts of family life in Edge Crossing, mirroring the ages

(Top) An older house. (Bottom) A lake-front home built on ancestral land by a married couple.

and interests of the residents. The yards surrounding the houses are all similar in appearance and function.

DOMESTIC PATTERNS

The daily household routine is organized to meet the human needs and routines of a variety of persons who are usually periodically absent from the home on a regular basis. The very young, very old, and some women spend nearly all of their time at home. Adult males, who often have more than one home in which to eat, sleep, maintain a wardrobe, and take care of biological needs, do not. The household pattern, organized around the needs of participants, is described through the daily activities that occur there.

Older adults who have accustomed themselves to retiring early often rise at daybreak, but daily activities begin when children rise at 7:00 A.M. and get ready to go to school. Because the sleeping patterns of most adults fit their work schedule, they are often asleep when the children arise. The female head of the house usually gets up to see the children off to school and prepares breakfast for preadolescents. Some students prefer to prepare their own breakfast and others go without. If the woman is at work or has to sleep, a grandmother, aunt, high school age sibling or cousin, or another woman living nearby attends to the needs of younger children in the morning.

After the children are out of the house, other adults rise and are usually up by 10:00 A.M. Some have already left for work or to run errands by this time. Social, occupational, and educational schedules require that the household routine be flexible.

A meal is prepared around 10:30 or 11:00 A.M. by an adult female in the household. If the female household head is absent she leaves the food on the stove or directions for its preparation. The morning meal usually includes coffee, light bread, and grits. Pork cooked with peas, or bacon, pork chops, eggs, or fish are usually included in the menu. When the food is ready plates are served by a woman to those present and the meal is consumed in the living room, kitchen, dining room, or under a tree or on the porch. Family members position themselves for comfort, the desire to be alone, or to talk. Rarely does everyone sit together at a table. In fact, there are often too many persons present to share available table space. When members of the household come in during the meal or later and inquire about food they receive a plate, served by the woman. Friends who come in during a meal are usually not invited to share the food.

Children under three years of age are usually fed from the plate of an adult woman, although all adults offer little children food when they approach. Children over three years of age receive a plate and often sit at the kitchen table supervised by an adult female. After the meal is eaten the plates are usually abandoned where the meal was consumed, although women tend to take their plates to the kitchen.

Later, a woman gathers the dishes and glasses scattered around the house and takes them to the kitchen, where they are washed and placed in a drainer, or dried and replaced in a cabinet. Women attend to various chores after the meal—straightening the house, making beds, and sweeping floors. Clothes are washed at least weekly and usually more often. Sorting, folding, and ironing clothes is a routine housekeeping task which women perform for husbands, small children, and old or infirm members of the household. While women are engaged in housekeeping men sit talking to others, drift from the house, go to the Crossing store, to work, or to take care of business.

After household chores are done women usually spend several hours watching television, visiting, and tending to the needs of preschool children. Women usually have a small group of friends they see once or twice a week or one or two friends they see daily. They receive visitors informally in their home, walk to a nearby house, or if they have a car, they drive to the store to buy some items and then go to a friend's or relative's house. Women enjoy talking to other women about community news, children, and men, and do so by visiting or extensive use of the telephone. Most homes have a telephone which is in frequent use, particularly by adolescents. Telephone conversations vary from about ten minutes to two hours or more in length. There are many interruptions from children, television, and little tasks, but the content of the conversation is such that interruptions do not interfere with information transfer.

Another popular pastime of women is keeping up with the "stories," television programs which are broadcast from about noon until 4:00 P.M. Women, sitting on the edge of their seats, blocking out all other stimuli, concentrate on the "story." They discuss the events, predict outcomes, and take sides with characters on the screen during the commercials. Adolescent females hurry home from school, prepare a snack, rush into the living room, and join others involved in the program.

When the younger children come home from school, around 4:00 P.M., there is a lot more activity and noise in the houses and yards. Children from several households play or go to the store together. Children in elementary school do not usually have established responsibilities at home other than taking care of themselves, but in some households most of the housekeeping is reserved for older students, nearly always females. They are responsible for the routine housework after school and on weekends. They care for young children, wash clothes, iron, sweep, and mop the floors, burn the trash, cook, and rake the yard when needed. The distinct division between the activities of children and adolescent females, discussed fully in Chapter 7 and Part Three, reflects the different status of children and adolescents.

A second meal is placed on the stove in mid-afternoon and eaten when children and adults return to the house at dusk. The meal, eaten between 6:00 and 9:00 P.M., is usually served later in the summer when daylight lasts longer than during the winter months. The meal is served in a fashion similar to the morning meal but usually more persons are present. When family members are absent at mealtime some of the food is left on the stove for them to eat on their return. Rice and chicken pieces, greens with pork, macaroni and cheese, peas and pork, and fish and various vegetables are often prepared. The dishes from this meal are sometimes not washed until morning if females in the house are tired or are going out.

When the evening meal is finished some family members "wash up"[2] or retire early and wait until morning to bathe. Other family members are intently watching television. Babies have either gone to bed or are tiredly moving

[2] Bathe from a basin of water.

from one lap to another. Points beyond the home, shops, stores, and homes of friends have drawn adolescents and adults away. When visitors are in the house they engage in watching television, talking, and playing with the little children. Men often have not yet returned home for the evening, but when they return they eat, watch television, and retire. The persons most consistently in the house during the day and throughout the evening are adult women, but they sometimes visit others in the evening if someone is present to take care of young children.

The activity in the house is at a low level by 9:30 or 10:00 P.M. because most of the children are in bed. One or two persons sit half-sleeping with the television as a talkative companion, but by midnight they have retired. Depending on where they have gone, those who have been out come in between 10:00 P.M. and 3:00 A.M. and go to bed. The late hours that men and many youths keep accounts for their lack of initiative in the morning and staggers the activity level in the households through the day, evening, and the night.

Household activities are organized so that individuals with interests and responsibilities away from home can meet them while fulfilling their needs at home. Household functions are carried out in a highly flexible manner but lines of authority are clearly defined. There are no tasks that are so strictly allocated by sex that they cannot be performed by either males or females, although most tasks are routinely done by women, who usually delegate responsibility to younger females and sometimes to adolescent males. Authority rests with an older female; in some cases the oldest female is too old or sick to maintain control. She usually abdicates her role to a younger woman, usually a mature daughter who assumes the position of authority.

The female authority figure in every house is identifiable through her behavior in her home. Often two or three women, each having a house "to boss," cooperate and share numerous household functions, lightening their "load." The sharing of work, goods, and personnel between related houses is common in all households and a daily pattern in others. When two or more women cooperate to perform household tasks their time is more flexible, permitting freedom to engage in activities beyond the home, but they do not forfeit their authority within their own house. The daily sharing of goods, food, child care, and other functions between three households is illustrated in the example below.

Domestic Transactions   Maxine, 72 years of age, heads one household; Brenda, her 45-year-old daughter, another; and Linda, her 27-year-old granddaughter, a third. The three women share child care, food preparation, laundry and ironing, transportation, and other functions. Their interactions reflect the flexibility of household function and composition.

The three women live within 150 yards of one another and visit daily. One of Linda's sons, eight years of age, sleeps, eats, and keeps his clothes at Maxine's but spends most of the day with his siblings at Linda's. Brenda usually lives alone but her brother Joe (Maxine's son) lived with her after he left his wife. He slept at Brenda's and ate at Maxine's until he moved in with a girl friend. Brenda is seldom at home because she works two jobs. Maxine frequently prepares food for herself, Douglas (Linda's son), and Joe, who stops in occasionally. Brenda and Linda often give Maxine food because she has a steady income of under $100 per month. She returns some of the food to them when it is prepared. The three women often eat together in the morning at one of their homes. Since Maxine's health is not good, Linda and Brenda often prepare food for her and check on her in the evening. Maxine often does Brenda's washing and ironing and periodically takes care of Linda's older children when Linda works. They in turn provide transportation and various services for Maxine.

Domestic Interactions   Related households often operate almost as one unit and movement of personnel between houses is without formality. Clothing, food, and some other goods are transferred with little regard to ownership. It is sometimes ambiguous where one household unit ends and another begins in terms of the functions and personnel of the household. The reciprocity between the three households described above is not unique. Women usually have relatives or friends with whom they regularly share goods and services.

The activity level in many households is very high as relatives and friends of various ages move into and through the house. Often there are few adult male participants in the household activities because men have other places in which to spend their time, but they usually eat and sleep in the household to which they are most closely identified. Sleep and work remove most men from household activities. Male students often work part time and are involved in sports requiring practice and games. Often the most active male participants in households are retired or in poor health. Men spend their free time interacting with other males in set events[3] and with females in pair events[4] in various locations beyond the home.

Men customarily spend their time beyond the home but have a recognized responsibility to the household. Women spend their time at home and have definable roles in the male domain beyond the home. Their activities reflect the spatial arrangement in the community and the traditional division of labor. Although both men and women work in capacities beyond the home, the customary division of labor permits women to exercise authority and independence in the homes and allows males to express their social position and importance in community institutions beyond the home.

Women recognize the tendency of males to congregate, talk, drink, play games, and spend their time away from the home. When men are away from home women say they are "in the streets." If a man is spending most of his time with a woman his family will state that he is "in the streets." A man's activities away from home are not completely known to his family. Their lack of information is a protective mechanism shielding his activities from scrutiny and gossip.

Men who have stable marital relationships spend more time at home than others but are still "in the streets" regularly, talking at the Crossing store, having a beer with friends, or attending to various part-time occupations. Although men do not spend much of their time at home, they are respected when they are there. Older children become somewhat quieter and subdued when they enter the house. Men play with and talk to children under three years old but spend little time with older children or adolescents. Women usually acknowledge the entry of their husband or adult male offspring. Married women often keep their husbands' desires in mind if they plan to be

---

[3] A set event is defined as an event between three or more persons in which one person initiates to the others (Chapple and Coon 1942:706).
[4] A pair event is an event between two individuals (Chapple and Coon 1942:705).

away when he returns. They plan meals to be prepared by others or leave food for them.

When men and women interact there is considerable nonverbal communication because "people talk with their eyes." When a man comes into the house more glances than words are exchanged. Women can tell what kind of mood their man is in by looking at him. Married women say that trying to keep a man happy is a "hard thing to go through with." They study his various weak points and learn to use them to achieve certain ends. Women do not back down when challenged by a man, especially in the home. Many women accuse men of not treating them fairly and trying to manipulate them by withholding money. It is a point of honor with women not to let a man "hard time" them. A woman will enlist the help of other women for child care and take a job to prove to a man that he cannot make her do whatever he wants. Women agree that they will always "be out ahead" of men because "while men sleep women think." In the home it is apparent that women are authority figures who strive for harmony and to maintain a home for their children.

At some points in the system males are more clearly dominant. Stores and shops—the domain of males—are spatially separated from households, but the use of space in these locations has similarities to spatial arrangements in the house and yard. Houses are the focus of typically female behavior where men have socially defined roles. The stores and shops are a male domain and women have limited roles. The spatial distance between typically male and female domains reflects their role segregation. Because stores and shops differ in certain respects they are discussed separately; later their similarities and differences are compared.

STORES

The three stores in Edge Crossing serve an economic function and are important meeting places beyond the home. Stores are ordinarily open six days a week, including Sunday, and are not open in the late evening. The stock in stores includes various grocery items which are purchased for household use. In addition, beer, wine, and snacks may be purchased for immediate consumption. The clientele ranges from children about three years of age to the elderly.

Stores and shops are both male dominated, community gathering points. The most important difference between stores and shops are the reasons people go to them. Shops are organized to bring males and females together in a socially defined situation. Males engage in some of the same activities in shops as they do at stores but take advantage of opportunities to become involved with females. In stores and shops, women are customarily subordinate, and relate to males within socially expected parameters.

SHOPS

The two "shops" in Edge Crossing (see Figure 1) are similar in appearance and function to businesses throughout the surrounding area catering to enter-

The Crossing store on Saturday afternoon.

tainment needs in the evening. The plain but painted buildings usually have no signs indicating that they are places of business, although the clay or sand parking areas indicate that there is considerable activity there. During the day there are rarely cars parked outside, although one can sometimes go in and buy beer or snacks if the owner,[5] who lives in a house nearby, is around.

The interiors of shops are very similar. The building is one large room with a storage and service area in the back set off from the rest of the room. In the rest of the room there are pool tables, small tables with one or two chairs, a juke box, and space for dancing. These features practically explain the activities which are concentrated there on weekend nights.

At the shop persons of the opposite sex meet, business deals are made, and everybody acts the way he or she feels. It is also an important link in communication networks. Persons from other communities come to talk and hear the news. There is considerable travel between shops; cars filled with men, women, or both go from shop to shop in other localities looking for the best action, meeting new people, and finding out, generally, what is going on and where. Individuals and groups travel over two counties to a place where they hear that something interesting is happening. Often a band with a good reputation is playing and people from a radius of 100 miles or more attend. Even if the reputation of the band is not outstanding people go to hear it if nothing more interesting is happening closer to home.

The activity in the shops is fast moving. People meet, talk a while, decide they like one another, and move out to find more privacy. Often events which have occurred away from the shop are brought to a head and worked out. Consequently, quarrels which have been brewing between men or women over a member of the opposite sex are resolved by a show of force. Disputes over business or money matters are brought out in the open. When fighting,

[5] Most shops, including the two in Edge Crossing, are owned and operated by blacks.

shooting, or knifing occurs the police are sometimes called. Most shop customers try to avoid contact with police. They do not want to serve as witnesses, and less still do they want to be taken to the station. They do want to know what happens so they can relate their version of it to others. When it is clear that the police will be called, or that an innocent bystander may be shot, the shop becomes vacant within minutes.

The use of space and social forms in stores and shops, dominated by males, and in female-oriented homes demonstrates the division between male and female role that prevails in Edge Crossing. The use of space provides males with legitimate claim on public areas while permitting females independence in private areas. In each of the areas discussed here—land use, houses, yards, daily patterns, and social gatherings—males and females function independently. Yet the division of labor is such that they are dependent on one another for the coordination of routine activities. The realm of work and finance explicates the interdependence of male and female and the realities both face in the white-dominated economy.

2 / Economics

The need for cash income requires that most adults enter the white-dominated economic system and obligates them to participate more fully in the economic institution of the wider society than in any other institution. The demands and expectations of employers and creditors conflict with the needs of community residents for income, recreation, and social relations. Youths express disdain for occupations traditionally available to blacks, but older persons, admitting that life has been filled with hard work, look back with satisfaction on modest achievements.

The relationship of community residents with the economic system has changed through the generations and various adaptations have occurred. Within the past five years alterations in employment policies resulting from civil rights legislation have opened some opportunities to youths that were unavailable to their parents. Yet, finances remain a problem for everyone. Women and men experience similar problems in the wider economic system and cooperate more fully in economic endeavors than in other areas. In this section the economic adjustments made by adults, the problems of entering the job market faced by the young, and the customary allocation of resources are discussed, but first, social and historical events resulting in the current economic base are presented.

BRIEF ECONOMIC HISTORY

A fundamental knowledge of farming and a need for success were characteristic of persons who initially settled in Edge Crossing. Although the land did not produce abundantly, the crops and natural resources provided for the families living there. Mines, located about three miles south of Edge Crossing, provided employment for men who worked 10 to 12 hours a day, mining and transporting onto rail cars a fine, white clay. Some of them worked there long enough to draw retirement and do so today.

The emigration of young adults, beginning in the 1920s and 1930s, continues today. Young men and women went to northern cities, including New York and Washington, D.C., to live with relatives or friends and seek work. When they became established they sent for siblings or other relatives. Although family members were gone for decades, they maintained ties by letter, telephone, and messages sent through vacationing relatives. Northern cities and relatives continue to attract the young, although a greater proportion of them are now settling in Florida cities. Everyone says that the reason that

21

young people leave Edge Crossing is the lack of jobs, but some leave for other reasons also.

In the 1940s and 1950s adults acquired transportation and were able to commute to University Town or County Seat to work. They were often able to find jobs that didn't require the arduous mine labor or the back-breaking work in the fields. As this trend became marked people quit farming in earnest. They bought their food and "come out ahead," at least in terms of physical labor. Some older residents, looking back with nostalgia, say that although times were good, no one would go back to farming or the mines, which closed a few years ago.

Employment beyond the community brought various changes in economic arrangements but the traditional pattern is maintained. Males usually work far away from home. Women contribute to the economic resources of the household through paid employment, but their primary identification is with family and household.

FINANCES IN EDGE CROSSING

Economic arrangements reveal the impact of the wider society on the community, the division of labor, and patterns of employment during the life cycle. Mature men and women bear the major responsibility for bringing economic resources into households and the community. An analysis of patterns of employment and economic responsibility of males and females reveals a division of labor and the spatial arrangements associated with economic pursuits.

Because there is no permanent, full-time employment available in the community, men and women work in the neighboring towns, primarily in the large health care and educational complexes in University Town. More jobs are available in University Town than in other towns in the vicinity and employment networks operant in the community lead most persons to positions in University Town. Extensive travel, about 50 miles a day, is a requirement for most employment, adding more than an hour to the eight- to ten-hour work day.

The division of labor is reflected in the occupations of men and women and in their roles in the household and community. Males have a wide variety of occupations clustered around custodial, construction, and farm work. Some men's employment requires staying at the work site, permitting them to return to Edge Crossing only on weekends and during periods of unemployment. Women, employed in jobs reflecting their expertise in household management and child care, work as domestics, custodians, nursing assistants, and in cafeteria service.

Neither men nor women have high incomes but men fare considerably better in wages than do women (U.S. Census 1970: Count Four). Men are usually more regularly employed than women and often work at more than one occupation. Although the four school teachers in Edge Crossing, all female, probably have the highest incomes for persons working one job, men often have full-time jobs and various part-time occupations. Women, restricted to employment expressing their domestic identification, often work only part-time or temporarily. Personal and family economic crises resulting in unmanageable debts often cause women to enter the work force. When the crisis is resolved, bills paid, or incomes from males or welfare established, they quit work. Some, working as domestics in nearby communities, have held the same part-time positions for years.

Employment in the wider society reveals several patterns. Permanently employed men and women work in unskilled and semiskilled occupations and receive low remuneration for their efforts. Women maintain stronger ties with home, more often work part-time or temporarily, and work in positions related to their traditional roles. Males are more actively involved in economic pursuits in the wider society, have more varied skills than women, and pursue more than one occupation at a time. Everyone finds it difficult to cope with jobs and they often "get hot" (angry) about the demands of employers. Usually residents have few alternatives in employment situations when they feel wronged. They can leave the job, blow up and beat the offending party (frequently discussed but rarely done), or quietly do the job as demanded. Sometimes they choose to leave the job, "just walk off," but in most cases they do as told to "get along." Work frustration is prevalent and everyone knows that he has to "bite his lip to get along" sometimes.

Within the community the resources gained through employment are distributed to others. Women usually have only one paying occupation which may be located in the community. Baby sitting, at the rate of $2.00 per child daily, is one source of income for women whose household responsibilities or personal involvements prevent other employment. In many cases women too old to be in the work force or having children of their own take care of children. Payment for baby sitting is in cash, goods, services, or a combination of the three. Although income from baby sitting is not high, there are few expenses associated with it.

Another source of income, requiring greater financial investment, is transporting persons. Transportation is an expensive necessity for those who do not have adequate incomes to maintain automobiles. Women who own or have access to cars "carry" persons for payment. For example, every woman needs to go into town at least once a month to "trade" (grocery shop and pay bills). A ride into University Town or County Seat costs $5. The rate drops to $2 for a trip to the smaller towns about six miles away. Although most employment is in University Town, most women "trade" in County Seat because food stamps have to be obtained there and most of them have long-standing accounts in County Seat Stores.

The state welfare department is a source of income directly available to some females (and a few males) in the community. Many people prefer to stay off welfare because welfare workers ask too many questions, make too many demands, and periodically threaten to discontinue the payments. But others find welfare less troublesome and more dependable than the work they are able to get, and they make their peace with the intrusions of welfare workers. There are several sources of welfare income in the community, including aid to dependent children, disability checks, and old-age assistance. Aid to dependent children is the most prevalent and amounts to about $55 per month per child. Disability income depends on the percent disability allowed by the state, while old-age assistance is about $85 per month.

Welfare recipients are also eligible for food stamps, stretching income at the grocery store. Women often receive food stamps even though one or more persons in the household are employed, because the family income is low, dependents are numerous, and they meet eligibility requirements. Children in most households are eligible for free or low-cost lunch programs. Women exploiting income opportunities in the community are restricted to sources that permit other responsibilities to be met. Baby sitting, transporting persons for payment, and welfare are among the most important.

Men, unrestricted by domestic responsibilities, often work fulltime and have other sources of income. They have extensive personal networks into neighboring black communities resulting in various part-time occupations (called "side hustles"). Construction work, sale of fish and farm products, and delivery of goods to points beyond the community are occupations resulting in cash payment.

Males' and females' incomes are distributed into household budgets and into various personal networks. In household financial arrangements there is an emphasis on males *giving* money to females. When assistance is not freely given, women assert their independence of males, take jobs, and "get along" without them. Ideally, married couples collaborate on a household budget, but in fact, men keep as much money as they need and give the rest to wives, girlfriends, and mothers. Women rarely know the exact amount of men's pay because men receive cash from various sources and cash the check from their "steady" job. Cash, in amounts up to $20, frequently transfers among adults. Males often contribute to more than one household, giving between $10 and $50 per pay period to a mother or girlfriend. When they are married their gifts to other women are reduced and more money is given to their wives. Generally, women acknowledge a man's responsibility to his mother and expect him to "give her a little" from each pay check.

Men, who tend to have more money than women, are usually gift bearers, but women frequently assist their boyfriends or sons when they are "short." Older women, typically dominant household heads, receive cash from several persons and lend "a little money" to younger relatives when requested. The pattern of reciprocity involves males giving cash to various women who, in return, provide housekeeping, laundry, meals, and other favors. Women receive cash from a variety of sources, including sons, fathers, husbands, boyfriends, and their own employment; they mastermind the family budget.

Household budgets focus on payment of the bills for electricity, telephone, mortgage on home, car, groceries, and accounts at stores where clothing and other goods are purchased. When only the man in a home is working he gives part of his pay to women (wife, mother, or girlfriend) to pay the bills. Working women, who receive some income from males, first pay the bills mentioned above and usually also spend money on clothing, household furnishings, and entertainment.

Financial worries are cited among the reasons that most men and women feel the need to get out of the house and have a "good time" on the weekend. Paradoxically, a portion of the weekly income is spent when men and women go out, drink, and forget their troubles for a few hours. Nearly everyone agrees that if you do not forget your troubles once in a while you "go crazy" and that is worse than being "a little short" at the end of a pay period. Most women who have "a house to boss" do not go out very often and are very responsible about their financial obligations, including helping kinsmen when they need assistance.

Despite careful planning there are often economic crises that require cash transfers greater than the small amounts that are customarily exchanged between friends and relatives. Major economic crises are handled through short-term loans from relatives and are usually repaid within a month unless different arrangements are made. Major economic crises include travel expenses, car repairs, and overdue car payments and are usually paid in cash.[1] Financial assistance of various sorts is usually expected among kinsmen. It is expected that when assistance is freely given that the receiver will "do something" for the giver in due course. Parents and grandparents customarily help their children, and siblings provide assistance for one another for major purchases including "getting a place to stay" (a home). In some cases, financial aid extends to cousins, nieces, and nephews, but usually dependence is upon closer kin.

There have been some changes in the economic opportunities available to blacks but older persons think only in terms of the traditional, low-paying positions they have had. Most adolescents begin their working lives in the community and later enter the job market in the wider society. An analysis of adolescents' experience in the job market reveals the problems faced by most community residents.

ADOLESCENTS AND THE JOB MARKET

Adults tend to protect adolescents against the realities of employment because they feel that work in the wider society is an unpleasant necessity of life. Most youths try to move into job opportunities in the wider society after they leave school, but are employed first in the community. High-school-age students work at the church camp ground (black) when it readies for summer opening and are paid about $10 daily. They rake leaves, clean cabins, repair buildings, and do some building construction. The Office of Economic Opportunity program in the community employs about 20 adolescents in the summer to clean the school yard and supervise younger children in the summer educational program. These jobs are welcomed by youths but their earning capacity is restricted.

Young persons seeking employment in the white-dominated economy encounter numerous problems. Many high school graduates stay at home for several months or a year or more before securing employment outside the home. Fifteen students who graduated from high school in June stayed in the area but none were employed by September. By December, four had secured jobs and two of them had already quit working. Most young people have difficulty finding a job that they want to keep. Many enthusiastic high school graduates' hopes are dashed against the reality of discrimination, inability to perform on standardized tests, and parents who tell them what kind of employment they can get. For example, Dean felt an urgent need for a job immediately upon graduation in June. She enlisted my help in locating one at the end of May. My role was to take her to various locations where she had heard about openings or to answer advertisements listed in the University Town newspaper.

[1] In the community the economy is based on cash. A few persons have savings accounts but checking accounts are almost unheard of.

We set out one morning; Dean was filled with high hopes. Before we returned late in the afternoon she had responded to 18 advertisements and leads. She applied at the Veteran's Administration Hospital as a nursing assistant, at the University as a nursing assistant and clerk typist, and for a wide assortment of food handling and office positions in town. The University and the V.A. required exams and she scheduled to take them a few days later.

By August, Dean still did not have a job. She failed the civil service exam, and took the state exam twice unsuccessfully. When she applied for waitress positions she was told that they had already been filled or that they would call her. Yet the ad would run in the newspaper for several days more. Dean and I spent all day answering ads and trying to decide what she should do next on three or four occasions. In September she asked me to help her look for a job "one last time." She was responding to three ads for waitresses. At the first two places they told her that they had already filled their vacancies. I waited in the car as she went into the third restaurant located on one of the main streets in University Town. It was large, well-maintained and served moderately priced meals to a clientele of high school students and university personnel. Dean returned to the car in about ten minutes with a job. I do not consider it coincidental that the restaurant manager was a "soul brother."

Dean worked happily at the restaurant for four months. Eventually, three factors resulted in her leaving the job. She was committed to taking care of her sister's baby while her sister attended school, she became sexually involved with her boss and did not want the relationship to conflict with work, and she wanted to visit friends down state frequently for several days at a time. By the end of March, following her graduation nine months before, she had not located a job compatible with her other responsibilities and interests.

The personal lives of many young women are complicated, contributing to job instability. After a few years of switching jobs, staying at home, or working part time, some women find a job that fits their life style. The cafeteria and kitchen at the University Hospital employs a large number of black women, including about ten young women from Edge Crossing. They pool transportation resources and have developed *esprit de corps* on the job. Working in the kitchen has certain advantages although the pay is low. These women keep up with community members in the hospital as patients and perform various services for them.[2] Working with familiar people and seeing various acquaintances passing through the cafeteria makes work interesting. Job training takes place after hiring so that those who quit may be rehired there because they do not have to be retrained.

The process of finding and keeping a job is difficult because it requires dealing with the demands of white supervisors and adaptations in personal patterns. Many people find the necessity of working hard on their "nerves" and do not remain at one occupation for over six months. The fear of failure, and the possibility of it, is great. Consequently, most Edge Crossing residents adjust to jobs which demand far less than their potential.

Economic problems faced by most residents are partly a result of the social organization of the wider society which has held blacks in low-paying employ-

---

[2] For example, a young, pregnant woman from Edge Crossing was hospitalized, placed on a low sodium diet, and served eggs. In the presence of visitors she said, "Now how you think I eat egg and no salt." Within five minutes a cafeteria worker, a community resident, appeared with several packets of salt. The meal was consumed with proper flavoring.

ment situations. Youths usually have little preparation for encounters in white society prior to employment and some of their problems arise from the lack of employment-related skills available at school. An analysis of the educational system describes the impact of formal education on youths in Edge Crossing and suggests some of the reasons they have difficulty obtaining jobs they want.

3 / Formal education

The use of space, economic arrangements, and the social forms discussed in earlier sections indicate that Edge Crossing is a community having relative independence of and little integration into white society. The lack of access to the resources in the wider society is related to the educational system and the community's utilization of it. In Edge Crossing most learning occurs in situations separated from the formal educational system. The important lessons of life are learned in the home and community, yet the schools are a major source of skills needed to attain jobs valued by youth. The learning environment offered by the formal educational system and the interrelation of children and youth in it are discussed in this chapter. The focus is on education in schools and school-related events rather than on education in the home, a later focus.

Schooling as a process separated from home has a long tradition in Edge Crossing. Around 1900 students attended class three months a year in a church building. By 1925, there was a school building in the community located near the Crossing store, successively replaced by two others over the years. Currently the school building reflects considerable neglect from the county. Broken windows remain unrepaired, the septic system does not function properly, and the heating is often deficient. Informants say that maintenance has always been a problem.

During the 1960s there came free choice, the opportunity for black students to attend all-white schools. Not one of the parents in Edge Crossing chose to send his children to the white school. Parents explain that they wanted their children close to home while at school and that the community school was satisfactory. Perhaps they did not want their own children breaking racial barriers or being scorned by their black friends as considering themselves too good, or "uppity," and attending a white school.

Complete segregation continued until eliminated by court order in 1967–1968. Elementary students are bussed to a school seven miles northwest of the community while junior and senior high school students attend school about nine miles to the east. The white school south of Edge Crossing is closed and the students attend school with those from Edge Crossing.

The formal education system, as it affects the children of Edge Crossing, takes them away from the immediate locality for most of the day during many years of their youth. The only exception to this is the Headstart program which has a classroom in the old school building. The voluntary program, in its fourth year of operation, is designed to give four-year-old children experience with a learning environment before the school years. Application must be

28

made for children to enroll in a program whose benefits are not apparent to all parents. Breakfast, lunch, and a wide variety of learning experiences are provided for the students.

The class of 20 students is instructed and cared for by a teacher and a teacher's aide. Volunteers, parents, and interested persons are invited and encouraged to come into the classroom and participate in the activities. The teacher and teacher's aide, both black, live in County Seat but are well prepared culturally, educationally, and temperamentally to work with the children and their parents. There is a cook who prepares meals for the students, a custodian, and a driver who transports the children to and from school. All three are local women.

The tasks which the class focuses on initially are not consistently practiced at home before enrollment. The children are taught to wash their hands, brush their teeth, blow their noses, and cover their mouths when they cough. The teachers encourage students to bring their problems to their attention instead of crying, biting, hitting, or kicking other children. Most of the children spend much of their time with siblings and other children. They are taught hygiene and manners but often do not practice them when beyond the direct supervision of adults (see play group, page 67). The Headstart environment provides consistent supervision by adults who feel that hygiene and manners are important to the future educational success of the students. The teachers also believe that the ability to talk to and with adults is necessary. They encourage the children to speak when spoken to, and to look at the person to whom they are speaking.

The teachers speak softly to the children, encouraging the very quiet ones to talk clearly and lift their heads while addressing adults. To achieve this the Headstart teacher squats or bends over to a child's eye level and places her hand on the child's shoulder, saying gently, "Darlene, let me see your eyes." When eye contact is established, she queries, "Do you have a tongue?" The child smiles and nods affirmatively. The teacher continues, "Then, you can talk to me, tell me what you want." After Darlene indicates her needs, the

The school building in Edge Crossing.

teacher praises her saying, "I like you to talk," and hugs her. The teachers attempt to subdue the activities of more boisterous children by assigning them tasks requiring physical activity, by constant reminders to sit down, by directing their attention to the class' current activity, and by praising quiet activity verbally and physically. In the course of the school year the students master many tasks and new experiences. The Headstart program is the first experience children have with formal education, and the only formal education they receive in their own community. Later, they attend school beyond the community and learn to cope with teachers and school situations that are considerably different from the experiences provided for them in the community.

The literature on formal education for low-income groups in the United States reveals patterns present in the schools attended by children in Edge Crossing. Public schooling is designed primarily to provide middle-class children with a knowledge necessary to compete for skilled jobs or college.

School teachers, as college-prepared professionals, usually accept the purposes of public education and unconsciously make decisions about the abilities and qualifications of students to perform in school and economic pursuits. Much has been said about the strong middle-class values in the classroom. Leacock (1969:205) suggests that it is not so much the imposition of middle-class goals in the classroom that affects low-income children but that teachers' middle-class values define these children as inadequate and the teachers lowered expectations are expressed by a "low emphasis on goal-setting" altogether.

Learning necessary for future employment is the accepted emphasis in public education. Blacks realize that opportunities open to them are limited, and respond to the school situation consistent with their perception of their future adult roles. Ogbu (1974:254–255) states,

> . . . blacks responded, more or less unconsciously, to this limited postschool opportunity partly by reducing their efforts in school tasks to the level of rewards they expect as future adults of American society. In the past this mode of adaptation, which results in a high proportion of school failure, served some needs of blacks as well as those of the dominant white society. For blacks it reduced the painful feeling that they worked as hard as whites in school for fewer rewards from society.

The literature suggests that the educational process is frought with a self-sustaining pattern of mismatched expectations by white professionals and by blacks' expectations of the system and themselves. Blacks desire the opportunities education customarily offers to whites. The schools provide programs designed for students with middle-class backgrounds and lack interest and relevance to the black students' experiences. Teachers expect and predict that the students are incapable of achievement (because of their backgrounds) and set lower expectations. Blacks anticipate the attitudes of the teachers, find them true, and reduce their own efforts. Teachers and the school system respond to these behaviors by creating and promoting programs and courses intended to be remedial, but they result in students having insufficient skills and knowledge to compete for jobs, just as standard curricula do. The cycle begins in elementary school and has predictable outcomes by the termination of the students' formal education.

By the time students are high school age they have usually turned their attentions away from the academic content of the school curriculum and have developed other interests associated with the school. Many remain enrolled because of these other interests.

The black students attend school, go to school events, and mix with whites while they are there. Blacks participate to a great extent in extracurricular activities, especially sports events and dances. Football, basketball, and baseball games played on Friday nights are well attended by all age groups in the community. Everyone knows the local boys on the teams, their parents, and their families. They cheer, socialize, and talk to everyone else at the game. Clusters of blacks and of whites sit in the same bleachers. There is considerable talking and joking among white and black youths but not much contact between the adults.

The convergence of white and black behavior was highlighted at one football game which Greg, a graduate and former football player, attended. He exuded school spirit; his voice carried well and he cheered often. He climbed up on the bleachers where about 150 persons, black and white, were seated. On the field an important play was about to be made. Greg faced the seated crowd, raised one fist in the air and shouted, "Is you ready?" The crowd responded, "Hell, yes." Greg reflected for a brief moment, hand over mouth, then changing the words but not the message, he yelled, "Are you ready?" The crowd noted the change, laughed, and responded louder, "Hell, yes." He repeated the two forms of the message again, receiving a more enthusiastic response each time, and then went on to lead the crowd in the rest of the cheer. Greg, like many of the youths, notices the difference between white and black behavior, including language, and sometimes modifies his behavior.

Sports events, emphasizing the masculine role, contribute to the unity of blacks in school-sponsored events and in local communities. Local teams made up of males ranging from 15 to 45 years of age play other teams from neighboring black communities on Sunday afternoons at the community playgrounds. Players are widely known and highly praised for their abilities. Community members, particularly adolescent girls and young women with children, attend the games and cheer wildly when local players make decisive plays. Ball games associated with school draw a more varied crowd, the entire family leaving home for an evening to mingle and interact with others. The ritual behavior at sports events, stores, and shops expresses male dominance and female support in public areas. (The roles of males and females in ritual is also dramatically revealed in religious ritual, discussed in Chapter 4.)

Ball games and other ceremonial events such as graduations and dances are the main events which attract attention to the schools. The emphasis placed on sports stands in contrast to the interest in the academic curriculum. The curriculum is not appealing to students and there is little effort to adapt classroom instruction or to involve students in academic endeavors outside the school situation. Most students seem content with mediocre grades, and often stay at home or skip school one day every week or so. Students stay at home when the opportunity to work for pay arises, a sick sibling or relative needs attention, or something unpleasant is expected at school. The practice suggests that students respond, often unconsciously, to the limited postschool opportunities by reducing their efforts. Figures for the nearby high school indicate that in 1972, more than half of the black freshmen left school before high school graduation but only one-fifth of the whites left.

Students from Edge Crossing socialize to a limited extent with white students. According to black students in the community there is harmony at school although problems develop occasionally. Black students protested because "soul" music was not played at school dances. One afternoon a bus driver would not permit black students to board the bus (the reasons were not specified by informants). This caused an uproar among students and about 30 parents who confronted the principal. The bus driver quickly relented. However, local students, teachers, and parents always stress that integration was in no way a difficult adjustment. They say that they have always known white people and have gotten along well with them.

Despite the organization and underlying purposes of the school curriculum and the students' response to it, many youths eventually enroll at the junior colleges in University Town or County Seat. Attending junior college to learn skills and knowledge to secure a "good" job is attractive. At junior college financial aid is often available; students may live with friends or relatives in town or commute daily. Some of them eventually finish college, contributing to the pool of college-educated people in the area who are often better educated than is required in their occupations.

Educational levels are not uniformly low; over one-third of the adults in the area have attended college (U.S. Census 1970: Count Four). Interestingly, nearly four times as many females as males have one or more years of college. Many students attend junior college because they have had "disappointments" on the job market where they could not secure employment commensurate with their desires for income or prestige. Students experience a double-bind in the economic and educational systems. They cannot secure good jobs because of their past education and the realities of the job market, yet they continue in the educational system hoping to eventually rise above the built-in barriers to comfortable incomes.

At junior college various opportunities do develop, even though they are usually not economic. Youths attending junior college meet students from the town and the entire junior college district. Relationships are widened, alternatives for entertainment are increased, and leisure time is spent in a greater variety of places. Youths in junior college participate less in community activities, although they keep up with local people through occasional social interactions, peers who live in the community, and relatives. Still, admission to junior college may be the first step toward moving into town, getting a job, and lessening interactions in the rural community. It is sometimes an avenue of access to jobs outside the community and is an introduction to whites and white values where students learn the roles they are permitted in the wider society.

Many young women who choose to go to junior college take a business course. They aspire to clerical jobs in which they can dress fashionably, meet the public, receive relatively good pay, and work in clean, pleasant surroundings. Others, who want to become teachers, plan to continue their education at the nearby state university or to attend the predominantly black state university located about 150 miles to the northwest.

Males, whose social status is tied to their economic resources, often experience the need for an income in mid-adolescence. They often seek employment when they are high school age and are not discouraged from doing so by their families, who have little economic surplus. Young men's incomes usually supplement the household budget, but even if this were not so, their working would diminish the stress on household resources that their membership creates.

As young men experience increased stature provided by their financial resources they move toward full time employment and away from the formal educational environment. Young men, valuing income, often secure jobs in pulp wood or harvesting operations which often pay well but are usually temporary. Males less often see school as an avenue to secure desirable employment than do females. Girls more often aspire to teaching, nursing, or clerical jobs where school subjects appear useful.

Previous chapters examined the distinctions between typically male and female behavior in space use and economics. Consistently, females identify with household and children and males with community life and economic endeavor. These divisions are given expression in education through the emphasis on sports. The patterns relating to males in highly visible roles are seen in ritual; they are dramatically expressed in church services and are discussed in the next chapter.

4 / Community ritual

Although males and females fill different roles, various events bring them together, expressing their interdependence and resolving minor differences that arise through time. The attendance at and participation in sports and shops are presented as group events enacting patterned male and female behavior. Events, bringing large segments of the community together, are rites of intensification reinforcing and intensifying customary status and role. In this chapter rites of intensification[1] in the religious institution are examined.

Religion is characteristically supported by symbols, setting off conditioned responses in participants, and rituals, those patterned behaviors bringing the group together around common belief and practice. In religious institutions group symbols and ritual behavior promote restoration of equilibrium to groups which are unbalanced by disruptive interaction sets in other activities. Religious ritual, often carried out in a definitive social space, draws representatives of all personnel in the community together and reaffirms the bonds that hold them together.

Religious rituals in Edge Crossing are customarily carried out in churches, separated from other institutions in the community, with a schedule of rituals following the weekly, monthly, and annual calendar ordering other activities. There are three Baptist churches in the community, each with its own history of development and a different minister. Their spatial separation (see Figure 1) belies the interrelatedness of the churches and the interdependence of the members but they are reflected in the ritual calendar. Mount Calvary (see Figure 1) has services on the second and fourth Sunday of each month. On the third Sunday of every month, St. Peter's has a service. Oak Ridge has services on the first Sunday in the month. During months having a fifth Sunday, the churches rotate the services among them.

Church is the place where men, women, adolescents, and children come after relating with one another through the week in schools, homes, stores, shops, and work. Drawing members of all ages and from each institution it promotes harmony and goodwill among those who compete with one another, are separated socially or spatially, or grow weary of constant interactions within the same group. Church is socially neutral; participants behave in accordance with the symbolic and ritual traditions passed from generation to generation, and seek communication with their fellows.

---

[1] A rite of intensification is ritual performed in response to a crisis which arises from changes affecting all members of a group in concert (Chapple and Coon 1942:706).

The community's largest church.

Ritual expression in religion does not attract everyone in the community. Women, especially older women, attend church and participate in the services in greater numbers than men. However, leaders, ministers, deacons, and ushers dominate the ritual. Although children are usually equal in numbers to the men and women present, they participate in a limited way. During all services, except on fifth Sundays, the choirs are composed of 10 to 20 adolescent females and 1 or 2 males. The congregation reflects in many ways the activities of community members during the week. Males, who engage in their ritual in stores and shops, do not attend church in great numbers, but those who attend are in dominant roles. Adolescents, who enjoy song and dance, provide the music. Women assure the attendance of children and sit in the front seats of the church where the minister and other leaders initiate action directly to them. The personnel participating in the ritual express customary behaviors and roles, but much more too. Earlier, the function of religious ritual was said to be a rite of intensification; as an example, the fifth Sunday ceremony, in which the three community church memberships cooperate during months having a fifth Sunday, is examined in the following section.

THE FIFTH SUNDAY CEREMONY

By the time Sunday school is over, between 50 and 75 cars are parked outside the building. People stand in groups talking and others move inside taking seats and talking in hushed tones. The women are fashionably dressed, wearing makeup, hats, hose, and jewelry. Men and boys wear suits. At 11:15 or 11:30 A.M. the choir sings a song signaling the beginning of the service and those outside move into the church.

Women and children take seats in the center front of the church; males tend to remain in the rear, near the doors, and some of them do not enter the church at all. The ministers and deacons assume seats facing the congregation and await the end of the hymn. During the service the choir, an active and highly visible body, is located directly behind the pulpit. The leaders of the services, the deacons and ministers, are always male. Occasionally women serve as ushers but the deaconesses have no active role.

The service begins after the opening hymn with the congregation and minister reciting alternate lines of scripture. A collection of pennies, nickels, and dimes is taken up in baskets passed by the ushers.[2] Introduction of visitors, announcements of upcoming church and school events, and recent deaths and invitations to visit other churches are made by the minister and members of the congregation. The announcement of events in several counties reflects the communication function of ritual gatherings. The introduction of visitors (who are considered prospective church members) legitimizes their presence and participation in the ritual.

The hymns, prayers, collection, and announcements set the mood of the congregation for the sermon. The visiting minister, from one of the churches in the district, is introduced by the regular minister who cites his good works and dedication to his people. During the preliminaries, persons talk quietly, entertain children, and pass babies from one to another, but when the sermon begins a hush falls over the group. Noisy children are quietly taken outside and everyone focuses on the minister. The sermon lasts about 30 minutes and varies in content from service to service. All the other parts of the service serve to augment the effect of the sermon.

The minister begins speaking slowly, standing in the pulpit; his voice carries through the group as he pauses after each phrase. He takes a recent event, personal experience, or biblical passage as a starting point to demonstrate human frailty and the power of the supernatural. As the sermon takes form his voice becomes louder, he gesticulates with his arms, and the pauses shorten. His voice becomes emotional; the congregation begins to participate with feet tapping to the rhythm of his voice. "Amen" is heard from scattered members of the congregation. Momentum builds in the sermon, the minister gesturing with his arms as he paces across the elevated platform behind the pulpit. The pauses between phrases become shorter and sounds like "Ah" are inserted where pauses had been. Everyone focuses on the minister, following his movements with their eyes. Feet tap and heads nod to the rhythm of the minister's speech. "Yes, Jesus" and "That's the truth" are exclaimed by members of the congregation.

The sermon continues to increase in cadence and volume. The point being made is that belief in Jesus Christ can lead to everlasting life in heavenly bliss. It is the will of God that all sinners repent, become baptized, and join the church. Finally, the minister is perspiring, wiping his brow, gesticulating wildly and pacing across the elevated platform. Abruptly he stops, apparently near collapse. The church is silent. A deacon rises, picks up a straight-backed chair, places it in front of the pulpit, and stands behind it. Rarely, someone is moved to act on the message of the minister and comes forward to join the

---

[2] The collection helps finance the annual Sunday school convention held in the district. Note that there is an annual ritual calendar of events other than national holidays.

church.[3] Ordinarily, there are two or three minutes of silence before other activities begin.

The minister initiates action to the congregation through symbolic themes with which they identify. Expression is given to the commonalities of the group through the focus on religious symbolism, the minister, and religious belief. The mood established by the sermon and the minister initiating action in the group is altered following the sermon. Then, various individuals rise and initiate action to the minister and the congregation, reversing the order of action established in the sermon. They touch on the symbolic themes of the sermon and crises in their own lives. Individuals resolve crises through initiation in set events and experiencing the support of the group.

Persons who want to "testify" begin speaking slowly, and build up to very active bodily movements and speech. Moving about in front of the pulpit, they bear any kind of message.[4] When they become intensely involved another person, usually an older woman, rises. The assistance offered is physical evidence of the support they receive from their peers; the silence and attention of the congregation is mute testimony of their importance. The older woman follows behind the speaker, saying nothing, wiping her brow, removing eyeglasses, or physically supporting her if needed. Most members who are moved to speak are older women and they are assisted by women. But men are supported by men, maintaining the prohibition against intimate physical contact between the sexes in religious ritual.

After one or more spontaneous expressions a prayer is offered by a deacon who reiterates the essence of the sermon and interprets it in terms of personal experience or recent events. A deacon who becomes intensely involved in prayer is helped back to his seat by another deacon and sits in a relaxed, slumped position for several minutes before looking upward again.

Becoming involved in the sermon is an emotional experience. The participation of the congregation with the minister creates a feeling of oneness with God and fellow man. Church members say that they go to church to "unburden," to "let go," to feel "close to God." They are "moved" to say and do things expressing their true feelings. The release of emotional energy is an exhausting and relaxing departure from the control demanded by everyday life. It restores interaction rates by focusing attention on commonalities and similar status before sacred powers. The prayer and spontaneous expressions maintain the mood of the congregation but lessen its intensity before moving on to more mundane matters.

The second collection, taken after the prayer, expresses the importance of each individual's contribution and the active participation of visitors. A deacon often chooses a visitor to assist a church member with the collection. The two people selected by a deacon stand behind a table near the pulpit, facing the congregation. Singing, the choir walks in rhythm to the music down one aisle of the church, around the last pew in the rear of the church, and back up the other aisle. Then, each member places his contribution on the table and

[3] The convert stands facing the congregation with downcast eyes and is questioned by the minister who ascertains the prospective member's name, whether he has been baptized, and whether he is a member of another church. Persons can change church membership by letter rather than be baptized by immersion again.

[4] Difficulties with finances, alcoholism, spouses, and children and the solace and help found in relying on the Lord are common themes.

returns to the choir area. The ushers indicate to the congregation which sections are to follow the path of the choir past the table and back to their seats. Some persons have money they need changed. The persons behind the table count the money, make change, and separate the bills from the change as it is placed on the table. Everyone, including the ministers, makes a contribution. The two persons counting the money satisfy themselves that they have made an accurate count; they compare and come to an agreement. Then one of them states, "Thank you for the $72.95." [5] After a short prayer is said over the money the two return to their seats,[6] and the collection is taken to one of the back rooms of the church where a deacon guards it from theft.

The manner in which the collection is taken demonstrates the importance of each individual in the congregation. Their participation and contribution are central to the ritual. The collection returns the congregation to the realm of worldly responsibility and identification with status and role. The mood set during the sermon is dissolved as people talk again in hushed tones. After the collection the choir sings, there are closing prayers and announcements, and people stand, talk to one another, and leave the church.

The church service provides for the release of tension built up during the work week and renews bonds of friendship which weaken in the absence of interaction. It is a rite of intensification, drawing together spatially and socially disparate entities and expressing their symbolic unity. The use of space within the church and the order of action, reflecting the dominance of males, contributes to the symbolism to which the group responds.

The restoration of interaction and the renewal of social energy is incorporated in the ritual. The process is further developed in the activities after the church service. The analysis of these activities reveals the importance of religious ritual in maintaining equilibrium and social communication between individuals, families, and communities.

The fifth Sunday service permits various ritual specialists to perform their customary roles for a large group drawn from a wide area. The behaviors of these specialists and their ritual relationship to community process are discussed next.

RITUAL SPECIALISTS

Ministers and deacons lead religious rituals and draw participants together through identification with commonly perceived symbols. Deacons are always church members, community residents, and are the ritual representation of community males. Ministers, however, are not community residents and are chosen by the membership for their ability to communicate to the group and to relate to their symbolic representations. The unifying function of the min-

---

[5] The amount of the offering varies. On fifth Sundays the collection is substantially higher than on other Sundays, when it ranges from $18 to $30.

[6] The amount of the collection sometimes depends on the collector's skill. If there is, for example, $22.15 collected, a bid for contributions amounting to $23 is made. The money is collected by ushers and placed on the table. Then, there is a little over $23, for example $23.25. He makes a plea to make it a "nice even $25." He continues requesting money until the congregation produces no more. Many people feel that there is too much emphasis on money and resist pleas for added contributions.

ister in ritual and in the arbitration of disagreements is enhanced by his social and physical distance from the community. The pattern of ministers living in communities separated from the ones in which they preach suggests that they function as cultural brokers, enhancing the flow of information, goods, services, and fellowship among the communities in the area.[7]

On fifth Sundays their leadership role is supported by the district choir, which facilitates the communicative potential of the minister and functions independently to maintain communication among black communities in the area.

The equally active role of men in the choir, as contrasted with local church choirs, is a reflection of male roles in community activities and personal networks extending to black communities over a wide area. Although women are authority figures in their homes, they are able to allocate responsibility so that they can sing in the choir. The make-up of the choir gives expression to the networks of communication binding black communities in the district together.

Exchange of information of almost any sort travels through these networks. Information originating in a home in Edge Crossing travels through the wider communication network to nearly any other household in the district. News about job openings, fishing, evening entertainment, and sports travels from one community to another. Once in a community, the information travels to other households there. Information of a personal sort, including news about babies, marriages, shootings, knifings, law troubles, illnesses, and deaths are also transmitted along the networks, reaching widely separated persons.

The composition, activities, and networks of the district choir express the social function of religious ritual. The social aspects of church attendance are important to all church members. The exchange of information and mingling with others contributes to the feeling of unity in the community. The district choir is a collective representation of various communities that participate in fifth Sunday services.

THE CEREMONIAL MEAL

The fifth Sunday service is a collection of guests representing spatially separated communities who ritually enact their oneness. The role of local residents as hosts to all the participants is expressed through the activities that follow the service and continue into the early evening.

After the morning service a dinner is served by community women who each bring a large container of food. The menu provided is similar to the usual diet, but because of the large number of persons involved there is greater variety. Women who are active in church work, including deaconesses and deacon's wives, take charge of cleaning the kitchen, receiving the foodstuffs, and keeping the food warm. After the service they hurry into the kitchen, don aprons, remove hats, and serve the plates.

The partaking of food and the organization of the meal is highly symbolic. The participation of all expresses in a different way the cooperation and com-

---

[7] Black ministers in black communities are consistently described as leaders (Dollard 1937; Davis et al. 1941).

munication of the group. The contribution of foodstuffs from many community households links the ritual to the family and kinship structure and expresses the supportive role of women as nurturant, sustaining figures in the community. The collection of foodstuffs under one roof and its redistribution to the participants reflects the symbolic significance of resource sharing and subsistence seen in the household and community. The role of males as community and ritual leaders is seen in the seating arrangement according to status. The highest ranking members of the religious organization—the ministers, deacons, and choir—are served first and seated in the church dining room. All other persons eat outside, placing their plates on cars or balancing them on their hands.

During the repast, the participants talk, see old friends, renew bonds, discuss children, and interact with a large number of persons in pair events. The pair events and social interactions reinforce the effect of the service (a set event). The morning service, the dinner, and the afternoon service [8] all serve the same function but are enacted in different ways. The reduction of hostility, communication among equals, the expression of oneness, and social support of the male and female role are expressed.

Ritual expression in Edge Crossing explicates social forms found throughout the community institutions. The division of labor, the dominance of males in the community, the nurturant, sustaining roles of women, and the strength of adults in relation to children are all demonstrated. In addition, the emphasis placed on redistribution of economic resources, the relative lack of economic surplus, and the acceptance of emotional expression in socially acceptable forms is evident. Ritual provides a forum for the symbolic expression of community norms and values and clusters them in a circumscribed space where both sexes and all ages of personnel participate. The temporal rhythm of ritual intermeshes with the activities of participants in institutions throughout the community and beyond.

---

[8] After the dinner another service is held at 3:00 P.M. It is similar to the morning service but there are fewer participants. There is no encompassing concluding ritual, participants begin leaving after the morning service, and by the end of the second service the leaders and a handful of the faithful quietly go home.

CONCLUSIONS—PART ONE

Community activities reveal the division of labor by sex and the customary forms of behavior in public and private places. Independent function by males and females is seen in the use of land, houses, yards, daily patterns, and social gatherings. Yet in the coordination of routinized activities they are dependent on one another. In the economic realm women tend to remain in the home whenever possible while males have the responsibility for bringing economic resources into the community. Similarly, formal education provides males with the opportunity to excel in sports and for their achievements to be acknowledged by female age-mates and family. Females, more than males, tend to see formal education as a way to better employment opportunities. Religious ritual explicates social forms found in other community institutions. The dominance of males in the community, the nurturant, sustaining roles of women, and the strength of adults in relation to children are all demonstrated. In Part Two the kinship system, the organization of households, and the socialization of children are described.

PART TWO

Kinship, Family, and Childhood

The use of space, institutions, and ritual, discussed in Part One, illustrates the ethnographic present in Edge Crossing. Kinship, family organization, and childhood development, presented in this part, clarify the integration of family and community. Chapter 5 addresses kinship as an ambilateral system, emphasizing recognition of ancestors and the rights and obligations of kin. Kinship and family organization over generational time are described in Chapter 6 through events and relationships in one descent group, illustrating the flexibility of the system and the sharing of maternal role and child care among related women. In Chapter 7, childhood development, customary rights and responsibilities of kin toward children, and the interpersonal relationships of children with one another and with adults are analyzed. The discussion of the kinship system in Part Two and the previous presentation on the community prepare for the detailed analysis of female adolescent maturation in Part Three.

5 / The kinship system

The kinship structure in Edge Crossing expresses ancestral relationships with founding fathers and claims to land, residence, and domestic
functions. Temporal and spatial dimensions of kinship including patterns of
emigration, population, and residence influence descent-group formation and
membership. A descent group is defined as a living group of persons, tracing
descent from a deceased apical (see Generation A, Figure 2) ancestor, who recognize the leadership of the eldest person having claim to ancestral land in
direct descent from the apical ancestor. This definition includes only living
persons in the group, but linkages to deceased ancestors are necessary to establish claim to land and the interrelatedness between operating descent
groups. Functioning to insure their continuation, descent groups provide for
the needs of members and have flexibility in affiliation and rights and responsibilities. In this chapter the formation of and affiliation to descent groups is
examined. The alterations in descent groups occurring over generational time
are discussed. The function of descent groups in providing for dependent
members is then reviewed.

The history of Edge Crossing dates back 100 years when four couples
settled there and reared several children.[1] All of their children stayed in the
area, remained on family land, married exogamously, and had large families
(see Figure 2, Generations B and C). The grandchildren of the founding fathers are present-day older residents and they all trace ancestry alternating between males and females in ascending lines to arrive at apical ancestors.[2]
Affiliation to a descent group by tracing linkages selectively, through either
males or females in any one generation with a difference in emphasis, is characteristic of ambilateral systems (Firth 1957:5).

Descent groups formed around the founding fathers, their progeny, and
grandchildren (see Figure 2, Generations A, B, and C). When founding fathers
died, descent groups segmented and formed around their male and female
children, all of whom remained in Edge Crossing. Members of Generation C
(see Figure 2) emigrated[3] and left only one or two siblings on family land.

[1] Informants relate anecdotes about ancestors who were slaves, but their living arrangements, progeny, and locations of residence are unclear. This may be a product of the advanced
age of informants or the unsettled conditions of the mid-nineteenth century.
[2] Through the generations intermarriages between the four families have occurred. It is possible to develop a kinship diagram representing every person in Edge Crossing in some kinship
relationship to all others.
[3] Persons who emigrated produced fewer children, probably reflecting upward mobility or
the greater availability of birth control in urban centers.

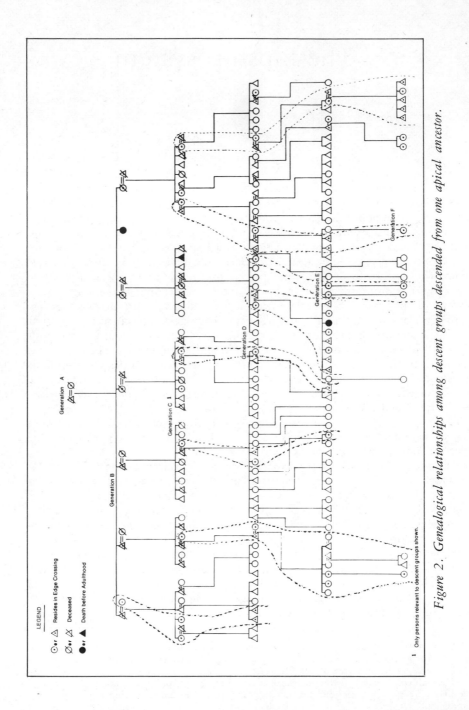

Figure 2. Genealogical relationships among descent groups descended from one apical ancestor.

Those who remained now head descent groups but maintain bonds with siblings who moved away.

The bonds between siblings are illustrated by the distribution of family land. Family land is divided among siblings at the death of parents but those who emigrate often forfeit their rights to land and permit their portion to be divided among their siblings remaining in Edge Crossing. Emigrated siblings who maintain kinship ties and assist in the payment of property taxes are allotted a portion of their siblings' land if they return to Edge Crossing to live.

Family land is held intact through many years by the payment of taxes by descent group members. The land is divided after the death of parents as siblings have need for it. Land holdings remain fairly large because most persons with claim to land do not exercise it when they live elsewhere. Land rights are established by descent group membership but tend to remain operational only through residence. Residence on family land before adulthood is necessary for descent group membership.

Most descent group members who remain in Edge Crossing build on family land before the death of parents, affirming their claim to it before it is divided. The clusterings of houses in Edge Crossing, discussed in Chapter 1, are a manifestation of the settlement pattern of descent group residence patterns. Most persons remaining in Edge Crossing live on ancestral land. Those who have left the area may return, but children born to emigrants usually cannot. They are not members of descent groups in the community and have not contributed to tax payments or other kin obligations there.

Rights to land in Edge Crossing are similar to those described for members of the *kainga*[4] in the Gilbert Islands.

> The original ancestor had lived on a certain tract of land. Some of his descendants continued to reside there but others moved away. Those who continued to reside there *plus* (author's emphasis) those who had been born and raised there but had moved away after marriage, formed the *kainga*. Thus those who were born on the land inherited membership even if they moved away; but if they moved away their *children* did not inherit membership. Thus, if a man's parents were living patrilocally he would belong to his father's *kainga:* if they were living matrilocally he would belong to his mother's. It was thus, in a sense, *parental* residence choice that determined the individual's *kainga* membership (Fox 1967:158).

Rights to land are dependent on descent group membership and the acceptance of responsibilities in the descent group.

The formation of a descent group occurs at the death of the eldest person resident on family land in direct linkage to a founding father. The largest possible descent group is composed of a living person from Generation C (see Figure 2) who traces descent from a founding father (through mother or father) and his (or her) children (Generation D), grandchildren (Generation E), and great-grandchildren (Generation F). In actuality no group is as large as theoretically possible because emigration has resulted in members of Generations D and E affiliating with descent groups (on the mother's or father's side) beyond the community. Most persons who emigrate do not return to Edge Crossing, thus reducing substantially the composition of operating descent groups.

[4] The *kainga* is a kin-based land holding organization.

Four characteristics of descent groups are noted (see Figure 2). Affiliation to descent groups alternates between male and female linkages to arrive at linkages with a founding father. Descent groups usually have representatives from three or four generations. The number of persons in a descent group is only a fraction of those who would have been members if they or their parents had not emigrated. Children of emigrants are drawn into descent groups when they are sent to Edge Crossing to live with relatives (on the mother's or father's side).

The formation and constitution of descent groups indicates that ambilateral descent (selectively tracing linkages through either males or females in any one generation) was established by Generation C (see Figure 2). A preference for emphasis on the male linkage is seen in the continuity of the male surnames,[5] and in tracing linkage to the male ancestor. In Generations B and C a woman, who customarily gave birth to children fathered by one man, married younger, permitting an easier identification of all her children with their father's descent group. In addition, farming, a male pursuit, was important economically. Now land is used primarily for householding and childrearing in which female interests are more important.

There is a tendency to choose affiliation with the maternal linkage in Generations D and E. It is a pattern for girls to give birth to one or more children before marriage. These children ordinarily maintain contact with, but do not emphasize, affiliation with the father's descent group. When the mother is married and residence is proximal to the father's descent group children do emphasize affiliation with the father's descent group. In certain kinship systems, notably those of the Maori, Tonga, and Samoa, the major emphasis is upon descent in the male line but allowance is made, so frequently it is considered normal for title to membership to be through females (Firth 1957:5). Descent group membership in contemporary Edge Crossing follows such a pattern.

Women, customarily having children fathered by more than one man, express a strong desire to live near their own kin and influence their children's descent group affiliation. Children who reside with maternal relatives, for example, usually maintain weaker ties with paternal links although they receive toys, clothes, and money from paternal relatives. When they are older (between 8 and 19 years of age) they can choose to live with relatives on the paternal side and affiliate with the paternal descent group. The system provides an element of choice for the individual although residence decisions are usually determined in accordance with the needs of the individual and group.

One of the major functions of the descent group is to provide for the needs of dependent members, both young and old. Residents state that children are "good to have" because they help take care of their parents in old age. Young women, perceiving the value of children, say "Kids is the keys to a lots of

---

[5] Until recently, the legal system required that a child carry the surname of the mother's husband or, if unmarried, the mother's maiden name, but differing practices have always prevailed in Edge Crossing. Single women and married women who have children fathered by men other than their husbands give their babies their maiden name or the baby's father's surname. The lack of conformity to the legal system is related to the kinship system, the disregard of impositions by the wider society, and the practices of lay midwives who formerly made out the birth certificates.

things." The system permits each generation to lead descent groups in maturity and to enjoy the status and authority leadership offers.

Children, necessary for the continuation of the descent group, are not solely the responsibility of their biological mothers. If biological mothers do not assume proper responsibility for their children's care women in the descent group see to it that arrangements for their care are made. Aunts and grandmothers who have the time to supervise children are their sociological mothers. The arrangement frees biological mothers to work or care for other children and permits the sociological mothers to have someone living with them. The significant role of women in descent groups is related to the value placed on motherhood (discussed in Part Three) and procreation.

The descent group also functions to care for infirm or old members. Mothers and fathers are cared for by their children. Usually a daughter or daughter-in-law lives with the parents in their house and other children provide financial assistance. When the parents die the child who has lived in the house and "looked after" them remains in the house. Often members of Generation C (see Figure 2) who have emigrated and have few children return to Edge Crossing when they are old and are cared for by their sisters. This pattern reflects the strength of ties between siblings who belonged to the same descent group in childhood.

The resources of the descent group are organized to meet the needs of dependent members and for mutual financial aid and assistance. Descent

A *descent group head*.

groups, composed of persons of various ages and both sexes allow the abilities and resources of all members to contribute to the group's welfare. The example of Maxine in Chapter 1 reflects the cooperation of descent group members from three households and four generations. Within the system each individual passes through dependent and independent phases in the life cycle and in the process receives more than he provides and provides more than he receives, balancing the support and assistance that flow between males and females of all ages.

The balance within descent groups is maintained by the options individuals have in affiliation. Children are placed with childless women by women with numerous children. Males and females marry, align with the descent group of their spouse, and eventually contribute children to that group. Older children, sent to live with relatives, affiliate with a descent group other than that of birth. Affiliation permits balance in situations where reproduction and marriage do not assure a normal distribution of personnel to a group.

In the next chapter, the organization of the descent group and household through five generations is examined. The formation of the descent group, the division of land, the allocation of resources, and the division of labor based on age and sex are discussed.

6 / The descent group
and household

The discussion of kinship and descent in the previous chapter indicates that an optative ambilateral descent system organizes kin relations in Edge Crossing. In this chapter one descent group is examined to illustrate several significant aspects of kinship, group formation, household composition, marriage, and responsibility within the descent group and household. The presentation focuses on the unfolding of events in a descent group and the meaning of these events to the spatial and temporal dimensions of development within households and generational time.

FORMATION OF THE DESCENT GROUP

Mary Jackson, 75 years of age and the granddaughter of one of the founding fathers (see Figure 3, Generation A), has spent nearly all of her life in Edge Crossing, but first left when she lived with a cousin in County Seat while attending high school. While she was away her brothers (see Figure 3, C1, C3, and C4)[1] were periodically absent working and engaging in courtship activities. Mary's sister (C2), about five years older than Mary, bore two children before marrying and moving to County Seat. Her sister became attached to her husband's descent group and died in childbirth with her eleventh child. Neither she nor any of her children ever returned to Edge Crossing to live.

After high school graduation at 18 years of age, Mary returned to her parents' home and developed a relationship with a young man from a community about 20 miles east of Edge Crossing. It is common for maturing siblings to move in and out of the household frequently for several years as they begin to work, court, and establish families of their own. During these years the composition of a household varies from week to week, although most comings and goings are by persons having established positions there.

Mary's courtship experience was similar to that of most women of her age and illustrates one of the differences between marriage then and now. She and Isaac, her boyfriend (C6), met at church and he came to her house to "call" on her. After a few months Isaac asked her if she would "keep company" with him; she agreed, and he approached her parents.

The meeting with her parents was formal; only Isaac and Mary's mother

[1] Letters and numbers in parentheses refer to Figure 3. The letter indicates the generation involved and the number refers to the individual on the diagram. Mary is C5 in Figure 3.

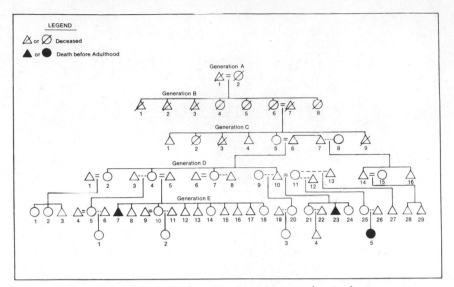

Figure 3. Genealogy of personnel in Mary Jackson's descent group.

and father were present. He requested Mary's "special company" and her parents consented. It was understood that her parents approved of Isaac as a potential son-in-law and gave him their assurance that Mary would court no one else. He agreed to see her at home and accompany her whenever they went out. It was believed that the "nature" of young people was to go out, enjoy themselves, and have sexual relations. Therefore, part of the agreement was that Isaac accept paternity and financial responsibility for any children born to Mary while he had her "company." Couples usually married when pregnancy occurred or after a courtship of a year or more. The parental role in courtship established sexual access and jurisdiction over progeny before marriage or residence changes.

After she and Isaac kept company for a year they were married in her mother's home, the same day moving to Isaac's mother's home to live for about one year. The following year they went to Palm Beach, Florida, to work with Isaac's brother (C7), who was involved in a harvesting operation. Although Mary was sickly for about a year after marriage she eventually became pregnant and returned from Palm Beach to live with her mother. Two years after her marriage she bore her first child (D2) in her mother's home. Isaac was living with his mother during the work week and spending weekends with his wife and her family in Edge Crossing.

Mary's four children, all delivered at Mary's mother's home, were born at two year intervals (D2, D4, D7, and D10). While her youngest child (D10) was two years of age, Mary had a serious illness and abdominal surgery terminated her childbearing. Mary, Isaac, and her children lived with Mary's mother, with or near Isaac's mother, and near Isaac's brother during these years, searching for a residence near relatives where Isaac could work. They finally settled in Edge Crossing when Isaac obtained permanent employment in the mine. Because resources to build a home were not available they lived with his or her relatives, who helped with child care when Mary worked.

Most individuals and couples move around when they are young adults and eventually settle near one of their parents after childbearing is well underway.

By the time Mary terminated her childbearing all of her brothers were married. One of them (C4) moved to a central Florida city and married. Another (C9) lived with his wife's family in a nearby community until he died as a result of a work site accident as a young man. The two other brothers (C1 and C3) obtained family land and built homes there. In Generation C, three of six siblings stayed in Edge Crossing, a higher percentage than in most families.

Isaac built a house on land Mary received from her mother in about 1934. Shortly after they moved Mary's father (B7) died but Mary's mother did not move into Mary's house for two years. Mary and her sisters-in-law "looked after" her in her own home until she had a stroke and could not walk.

Mary's mother had been the head of one descent group formed by Mary's and her brother's families. After the land was divided among them and her mother became dependent, the group segmented into three groups. They lived within 400 yards of one another and visited regularly. The sister and brother who left the area maintained ties there through Mary's mother and their siblings. Mary's brother (C4) who lived in central Florida had only one daughter. After his wife died he became sick and returned to Edge Crossing. Mary takes care of him in her home but his daughter supports him financially.

The formation of descent groups among Mary's siblings illustrates that males and females share in family land. Descent groups form around siblings who remain in Edge Crossing and claim the family land. Siblings who leave the area tend to lose claim to land but they often enjoy the benefits of membership as illustrated by the return of Mary's brother (C4) to Mary's household. In Generation C marriage was contracted through the parents and tended to be a permanent arrangement. Adaptations to marriage seem to have taken place; they are illustrated in the next section discussing the maturation of Mary's children.

SEPARATION OF SIBLINGS IN MATURITY

As children mature and develop relationships beyond the home in school, courtship, and work, the household gains and loses members. Before her children started leaving home Mary states that she experienced the happiest years of her life, although her husband worked 12 to 14 hours, six days a week at the mine. She and her maturing children took care of the home and Mary's mother and enjoyed long summer evenings singing and "jiving" on the front porch. The household composition was changed when she acquired two foster sons and her children started leaving home.

In 1937, Isaac's brother (C7) from Palm Beach requested that Mary take care of his sons. He and his wife had three children but he had a liaison with another woman who had two boys fathered by him, five and eight years of age (D14 and D16). The relationship had grown sour; she was drinking heavily and was taken to court for the custody of the boys. The father sought another woman to take care of his children.[2] Mary was reluctant to take the children but her brother-in-law "beg and plead so pitiful" that she consented. The next

---

[2] Mary stated that her brother-in-law's wife would not take the boys because she and her children were "mulatto" (light-skinned) and she did not want them in her house.

weekend the father (C7) brought the boys to Mary's house to live until adulthood. The placement of the boys in Mary's household illustrates the variety of channels through which kinship obligations flow. Mary was related to C7 through her husband and obligated to him because she and Isaac had worked for him shortly after marriage. Thus, the household was composed of persons related through the female line to a founding father but included two boys related to a male spouse.

The entrance of the boys into Mary's household occurred when her children were maturing and leaving home. Mary's daughter (D2) went to live in central Florida with Mary's brother (C4) to attend high school with his daughter.[3] When D2 finished college she returned briefly to Mary's home, married in 1940, and then settled in a western city. Although she returned to her mother's home for three months when she gave birth to her first child, she has never lived there since.

Mary's youngest daughter (D7) quit high school and stayed in County Seat. She married a well-established man about 20 years her senior who was a crew boss for harvesting operations in areas surrounding County Seat.

The only son (D10) was active in courtship and was linked to three girls by procreation, but did not marry. He left the community in 1951 when he was drafted. Indications are that D10 was a much-sought man because two girls designated him as the father of their babies. One gave her baby the Jackson name, but he denied paternity of either. Although the third girl designated another man as the father, Mary, the girl's mother, and D10 acknowledge him to be the father.[4]

In 1954 the son (D10) returned from the service and lived in University Town. He established a relationship with D11 who had two children (E25 and E27) from former relationships. One child (E21) was born to them shortly after their marriage.

Mary's second eldest daughter (D4) remained at home until she was over 25 years of age, periodically working away from home. When she gave birth to her first child she was assisted by Mary and "gave" the child to Mary because she did not want to marry the baby's father. After the birth of her second child[5] she married and moved to County Seat.

After D4 left the household only five members remained and two of them (D14 and D16) were often absent.

The separation of Mary's children at maturity reveals patterns associated with household formation. Girls often leave children born before marriage with females in the descent group when they marry and change residence. Women often receive assistance from their mothers at birth and return home if they are away. Children from a household usually leave to work, court, and live with other relatives while they are establishing independence of parents. Usually one or more children remain in the home, as D4 did for several years, and if they all leave one or more of them return after a few years. In the next section the return of Mary's children to family land, household composition, and function are discussed.

[3] Both of them graduated from high school and the black university in Florida.
[4] Grandmothers and other interested persons determine paternity by the appearance of the child and the admitted or observed activities of the mother.
[5] The second child was born on the same day that Mary's mother (B6) died. He died of influenza before one year of age.

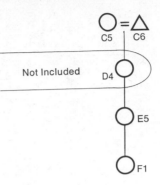

Figure 4. Mary's household in 1965.

HOUSEHOLD ORGANIZATION AND
DESCENT GROUP MEMBERSHIP

Flexibility, characteristic of kin-related behaviors in Edge Crossing, is illustrated in household function and the distribution of responsibility among related households. In this section the activities of Mary Jackson's descent group in 1972[6] are used to reveal the fluidity of household membership, the distribution of responsibility, and the membership of descent groups. The changes occurring in Mary's descent group pertinent to the discussion are briefly reviewed.

In 1965, Mary's son (D10) and her second (D4) and third daughters (D7) moved back to Edge Crossing. Each had a house built within 75 feet of Mary's home on family land. The compositions of the households about seven years ago reveal the personnel involved in activities in 1972. Mary's household was composed of four members (see Figure 4). One stepson had left because Mary did not like his drinking in her house. The other (D14) lived with his wife's family after the birth of their son (E28). Mary's granddaughter (E5) remained at home and gave birth to a daughter (F1).

The household of Mary's son (D10) included four regular persons and one who was periodically absent (E27). Before her marriage the daughter of D11 (E25) lived with her paternal grandmother in Edge Crossing. Her son (E27) lived in the household at times but stayed with his paternal grandmother during some periods (see Figure 5). Mary's second eldest daughter had 11 children, 10 of whom survived. She and her family lived in a separate dwelling (see Figure 6). The household was composed of ten persons (one of her sons [E13] was given to D7 and one daughter [E5] was given to Mary).

Within a year after the birth of D4's last child she became ill and was in a state hospital for 18 months. Her husband (D5) moved to south Florida and has never returned to the household. While D4 was gone all of her children moved in with Mary and D4 has not lived in her house since.

The youngest daughter (D7) lived with her husband and the boy (E13) given to her by D4. She separated from her husband and moved to New York. She placed the boy (E13) with Mary and has financially supported him ever since. After D7 went to New York, D14 and his wife moved into her house.

[6] I was present in Mary's household frequently and observed many of the events reported here.

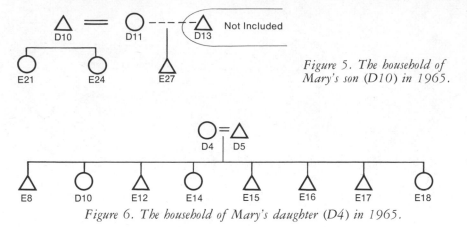

Figure 5. The household of Mary's son (D10) in 1965.

Figure 6. The household of Mary's daughter (D4) in 1965.

They had one child then and another in 1969. In 1972 their household was composed of four persons although D14 was often absent (see Figure 7).

In 1972 there were three households (since D4 and her children live in Mary's house) composed of 24 persons coinciding roughly with the descent group in Edge Crossing headed by Mary and Isaac. In the discussion below, the movement of personnel between the households and household activities reveals an accurate picture of descent group membership and household organization.

The flexible organization of the households and the groupings of personnel reduce the social boundaries between them. Household members group together according to age. The eight children in the play group spend their time outside. Four adolescent girls from two households spend their time in one of the three houses. The six male adolescents move in and out of the houses but are usually away from the houses except at night. The adults work away from home and often communicate to their children through Mary and Isaac, who are usually present.

Child care responsibility is shared among the women and adolescent girls in the households. There are only two children (F2 and E29) who have to be "looked after." When the adolescent mother of F2 was in school Mary, Isaac, and D4 were primarily responsible for her. When D7 visited over the summer she took F2 back with her and she has not returned.[7] Mary and Isaac are responsible for a four-year-old boy (E29) because he plays in Mary's yard and house throughout the day. Because his mother works, he usually eats at Mary's but goes to sleep in his mother's home under the care of his ten-year-old brother. All the other children are either in a play group or are adolescents. They are responsible for their own behavior but they are subject to the authority of all the adults in the households. The female adolescents in Mary's house are responsible for housekeeping and some food preparation. One adolescent daughter (E21) performs the same role in Mary's son's home but sometimes helps her cousins with their work at Mary's. The adolescents in Mary's household, both male and female, usually sleep and spend their time in D4's

---

[7] The transfer of F2 into the care of D7 is an example of a young mother relinquishing her child to another mothering figure. This process is discussed in Part Three.

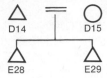

Figure 7. The household of Mary's stepson (D14) in 1972.

house but return to Mary's to eat, go to the bathroom, and watch television. The play group and adolescent associations cut across household lines, adding to the fluidity of personnel in the households.

Although the young household members are loosely organized in the homes there are core persons closely identified with each household. The core persons in Mary's household are Mary, Isaac, and their daughter (D4). In Mary's son's household, he and his wife (D11) are consistently resident. The wife of Mary's stepson (D15) is the stable adult in that household because her husband is often absent. All of the resident adults are in frequent contact with Mary and Isaac because they visit several times a day. One of the reasons for the constant interaction among the adults is that the only functioning bathroom, well, and telephone are located at Mary's house. All members of the three households share them. The three households would function as one unit except for two important factors. First, married couples have exclusive sexual access to their marital partners within the households and usually sleep in their own houses.[8] Second, the women in each of the three households usually cook one or two meals daily in their own houses. All other household functions and personnel are loosely identified with all of the houses and alternate between them.

Household composition varies as young persons leave to work elsewhere and to visit. For example, E10 and E13 stayed in New York with D7 over the summer and E14 stayed with her father in south Florida. Households also expand when young persons tangential to the households take up residence. For example, E25, the daughter of D11, sometimes stays at Mary's and so does the husband of E5. Household function is not disrupted by the addition or subtraction of one or more persons.

The three households function as a descent group in day-to-day affairs, but over time there are irregularities. When D7 went to New York she would have lost her position in the group; but she maintains membership by supporting E13 and taking care of F2. She still owns her house and returns annually to Edge Crossing. By every indication D7 is a member of the descent group although she is not resident in Edge Crossing. On the other hand, D14 and D15 are resident and enjoy the advantages of descent group membership. They receive child care, live on family land, and are treated as group members. But D14's claim to family land and descent group membership is very tenuous because he is not properly related to the descent group (see previous section) and his behavior has not endeared him to Mary. It is his wife who maintains the relationship with Mary and Isaac. She (D15) arranged for a home to be built on her family land and she and the boys moved there in December, 1972. Her renewed attachment to her family has defined her and her children as distinct from Mary's descent group but her sons (E28 and E29) still stay with Mary when she works.

[8] Married persons may also have other sexual contacts beyond the households.

A similar event is occurring with Mary's son (D10) and his wife, with different results. They have received family land from Mary and built a house across a lake from Mary's house. When they moved there they retained descent group membership because D10 is the only son and has assisted Mary and Isaac with house maintenance and in other ways through the years. Descent group membership and residence do not necessarily coincide. Persons living on family land do not always secure possession of it. Descent group membership is determined by linkages to founding fathers, residence, and maintenance of kin ties.[9] Household composition reflects the age and affiliation of personnel but there are core members who endure. The core members are adult women and couples. Children move between related houses and in youth leave to work or marry. Households tend to cluster so that vital functions, including child care, housekeeping, and cooking, can be shared by women of various ages. Mary, an experienced woman, supervises the care of children in three households but delegates the responsibility to young females. The mature women work and their children go to Mary's to eat, sleep, and use the bathroom. The adolescent girls assist in housekeeping and cooking and often unite to get their chores completed so that they can do other things. Household composition varies through time and functions to meet the needs of the members through sharing.

In this section the organization of households is analyzed. The flexibility in household composition and function permits children to have a variety of relationships and experiences. In the next chapter the experiences of children are examined more closely. Childhood socialization from birth to the onset of adolescence is described. The material is organized around the natural divisions accepted by mothers and the changing social relationship of the child through time.

---

[9] The system is pliable. If Mary and Isaac had not had a son Mary's foster son (D14) would have had descent group membership despite the lines of descent.

7 / Childhood socialization

In previous chapters household patterns, descent groups, and families were discussed. The fluidity of personnel in the household, allocation of resources, and the responsibility for child care suggest that the care of children is given high priority in the kinship system. Childhood socialization, development, care, and education are the subjects of this chapter. From birth until about ten years of age the child undergoes continual physical and social change. Adults and other children interact with children relative to their abilities and needs, encouraging certain activities and behaviors and discouraging others. Socialization is the interplay of the child and his environment resulting in his learning behaviors acceptable to the group. It is necessarily related to the changing physical development of the child through the early years of life. For this reason the discussion begins with the infant shortly after birth and progresses through childhood.

INFANCY

Infants are born into descent groups and households but their nurturance is a female function. Birth usually places infants in close contact with their mothers shortly after delivery. The exclusive mother-child relationship usually lasts from three days to a week, when they are rarely out of contact with one another. The mother, immediately available to meet the baby's needs, sleeps with him to assure that he is warm and that she is awakened when he needs attention. During the first week of life the baby sleeps most of the time; when awake, the mother interacts intensely with him. He is cleaned, fondled, held on the lap, rocked, talked to, and fed. When the baby sleeps the mother sleeps, rests, visits, and awaits the next waking episode. The baby is fed on demand and is offered milk whenever he awakens. When the infant urinates or has a bowel movement he is changed immediately. The baby is usually dressed in a diaper and shirt and covered with a light blanket in warm seasons. A kimono and socks or overall outfits and heavier blankets are added in cooler weather.

The infant's father and other kin and friends visit the mother in the hospital and at home.[1] They look at the baby, remark on his expressions, and inquire about the name and sex. The facial features and hair of the baby are described and some venture a guess at who the baby looks like. The skin tone,

---

[1] The father of the baby may not visit in some cases. These will be discussed in Part Three.

hair line, ears, eyebrows, eyes, nose, mouth, cheeks, and hands are used as points of discussion. Babies over six pounds are described as "big" and "fat," and are thought to be very healthy.

If the baby sucks, purses his lips, or gets his fingers into his mouth and eats moderately well when fed, he is called "greedy," a positive characteristic for a baby. When persons visit the mother and infant for the first time they usually bring something for the baby or promise to do so soon. New outfits, money, or articles for baby care are presented to the mother. When a woman has her first baby the gift-giving and visiting is more intense than after subsequent deliveries.

The new mother accepts praise and gifts for the baby shyly. She smiles, focuses her eyes on the baby, and says very little. The visitors maintain the conversation; they talk alternately to the mother about the baby and then to the baby. When someone asks how she feels, the mother invariably says "all right." The physical possession of the baby and the pride she feels in having given birth to him outweigh any discomfort she experiences. The behavior of friends and kin expresses the importance of giving birth. The infant, so pretty and interesting, is admired by all. The interactions and gifts reaffirm long-standing kinship and friendship ties.

A week or so after the birth many persons visit and look at the baby but touch contact with the baby is restricted. The father of the baby may hold, fondle, and talk to him but he rarely feeds, cleans, or clothes him. Often the mother's mother or other related females feed, clean, and dress the baby. Care of the infant is a valued task and only the mother and experienced females are knowledgeable about baby needs. Usually the mother has had extensive child-care experience but may not have handled a newborn. It is the role of experienced females to offer assistance and guidance when needed. Visitors and inexperienced persons do not handle the baby. The biological mother's sharing the care role with related women becomes pronounced later. Women often feel a closer bond to those children to whom they have given birth but they actively engage in child care of other children throughout adulthood.[2]

Three changes in behavioral pattern occur during the second or third week of life, reflecting the social and physical development of the child. First, there is greater acceptance of friends and relatives holding and feeding the baby. Second, the baby journeys beyond his mother's home for brief periods with reliable persons or the mother. Third, the baby is in the care of other persons in the home when the mother is away. Gradually the infant is in more frequent physical contact with others in and away from the home.

THE BABY

From about three weeks to fifteen months of age, several physical and social developments occur expanding the infant's experience. He learns to smile, laugh, verbalize some sounds, sit, stand, crawl, and is called "the baby." The

[2] In this discussion the term "mother" refers to the biological or sociological maternal person. The frequency with which females other than biological mothers assume maternal functions is very high and it is necessary to understand that "mother" may refer to one of several experienced women filling the maternal role.

baby's activities and responses permit reciprocal interactions with the mother, father, and family members.

The relationship the father establishes with his baby depends on various factors to be discussed in Part Three. In most cases the father assumes economic responsibility for the baby through support of the mother, sees his baby regularly, and takes great pride in his development. The interactions of father and baby are often brief but intense. The father holds the baby, kisses him, and talks to him in a low, soothing voice. The baby is held securely with both hands around the chest and sits on the lap when only a couple of months old. As the baby gains coordination he is held in a standing position on the lap and allowed to "jump" or alternately stand and sit, flexing the leg muscles. Other behaviors include holding the baby over head by extended arms and lowering him to the lap repeatedly. Keys, candy, or other trinkets are taken from the father's pocket to entertain and tease the baby.

During these interactions a constant stream of conversation interspersed with smiles and laughter occurs. The baby is examined, described, and his behaviors are discussed. When the baby is hungry, tired, or needs to be changed he is returned to the mother. The father of the baby usually demonstrates pride in him, relates to him in an affectionate way, and provides emotional and financial support for him.

The interactions of the baby are not restricted to the nuclear family. Siblings, grandparents, aunts, uncles, cousins, and other persons associated with the household also relate to the baby. Babies are indulged in every way but spend probably nine-tenths of their time with their mothers and other maternal persons in the home.

The baby sleeps with his mother by night and naps in the midst of household activities by day. He is fed whenever hungry and is sometimes offered food hourly. Most women feed their babies from a bottle and use one of the commercially available prepared formulas. Although fresh milk is usually not kept in the homes there is always milk available for the baby. The nutritional balance provided by these formulas or by breast milk helps account for the healthy and vigorous condition of babies in the community. Babies are encouraged to drink from a cup at about one year of age, although some continue to take a bottle occasionally for another year.

Babies are usually started on solid foods whenever they are not satisfied with a milk diet. Usually they are initially offered commercially available canned baby fruits. Most women do not use canned baby foods for more than a month or so, saying that they are not properly seasoned and that babies like table food better. By the time babies are four to six months of age they sit on their mother's lap and are fed from the plate. Peas, potatoes, cereal, rice, and other foods are mashed or premasticated to a palatable consistency. Babies are encouraged to express their desire for food and to feed themselves before one year of age.

Adult-baby interactions tend to support and develop sensual and tactile senses promoting sexual identification. Praise and reinforcement of typically male or female behavior is common during the first fifteen months of life and is increasingly evident with the passing of time. Throwing objects, striking others, and demanding, aggressive behavior of boys is praised. Girls are encouraged to climb onto the laps of males, beg them for money or candy, kiss them, and respond to their caresses. The behaviors of girl babies are described as "womanish" and those of boys as "mannish." The distinctions between expected behaviors of males and females begins almost at birth and gains momentum as the baby learns to perfect behaviors that are encouraged and rewarded verbally and physically.

Consistent with the general pattern of indulging babies, they are usually kept clean and neatly dressed. A daily bath and oiling of the body and hair are routine. The hair is brushed and flattened against the head. Girls have tiny plaits over the crown of the head to which ribbons are often attached. The hair of males is usually not cut for 12 to 18 months because some, but not all, mothers believe it physically weakens them. The mother's hands are pressed against the head in a firm, caressing action to "shape" the head. The index finger and thumb are pressed from the bridge to the tip of the nose encouraging straight growth. Legs, too, may be pressed daily to encourage proper development.

When there is a baby in the house, he is usually the primary focus of attention. He is played with, handled, and talked to and about almost constantly. A familiar person entering the house usually interacts with the baby before greeting or interacting with others present. The central position of babies results in their being contented, smiling, laughing, and responsive. They generally are not shy of strangers and are encouraged to go to the arms of a wide number of adults. Siblings and other children find intense pleasure in eliciting responses from babies. When permitted to, they present him with toys and hold, tickle, kiss, feed, and carry him.

The baby is allowed great liberty. Once a three-year-old sister sobbed to her mother that the baby had taken a trinket with which she was playing. The mother responded that the baby was *supposed* "to get into things." The sister had no recourse but to find other entertainment. Babies have license and need gratification during the first year of life such as they experience at no other time. Usually babies have mastered a number of motor and communication skills by 15 months of age. They walk, handle and request food, utter a few words understood by mothers, and interact effectively with various persons.

EARLY CHILDHOOD

The development of motor skills, especially walking and the ability to initiate and maintain interactions with others, gives the child greater independence and autonomy. Eating unassisted, bowel and bladder control, dressing, physical speech, and other behaviors are mastered before three years of age, diminishing dependency on adults.

Of the tasks mastered by the young child, walking is the most important because it allows freedom to explore the environment and to interact with others at will. Children often learn to walk before one year; they usually walk well by 15 months of age and are permitted outdoors to play in the sand and with objects, animals, and other children. The child's developing ambulatory and social skills provide opportunities for comment and praise from adults. A little child wearing an adult's shoes staggering across the floor brings comments, laughter, and physical support from others in the room.

Young children eat informally. The children usually sit beside adults at mealtime, eating from adults' plates or from a plate of their own, supervised by adults. There is little pressure on children to eat food items which do not appeal to them, but children are usually hungry and consume food whenever it is offered. Children often continue to take a bottle until they are about two years of age but can handle a cup and drink from it before this age. When children spill food or drink there is little comment. Children often carry food with them as they explore and interact with others. Crackers, bread, a bottle of juice or water, or candy are often held by little children as they toddle about the house.

There is considerable snacking throughout the day. The favorite snack item for children is candy. Candy is purchased from the nearby stores by older children or parents and shared with the younger ones. Soda is also a favorite with children and they can identify it and beg adults to share or open one for them. When permitted, little children can drink a 12-ounce bottle of pop but they usually drink water or juice. Children's consumption of milk is greatly reduced after about 18 months of age and sometimes earlier.

The informal, nonpunitive approach taken with feeding carries over into bowel and bladder training. Initial attempts to encourage bowel and bladder control are taken between one and two years of age. Most mothers obtain a potty which can be relocated in the house to suit the needs of both mother and child. The training process usually extends over several months. Gradually children learn to produce on the potty and are praised for their efforts.

When children become familiar with the expectations of others regarding the potty and can perform accordingly, they are permitted to wear pants at home. When they are traveling or visiting they are usually returned to diapers. Most children achieve bowel and bladder control during the day by the time they are two years of age but it is not achieved at night until a year or so later. When daytime control is not achieved until nearly three years of age, it is considered a reflection on the mother who has not taken the time to train her child.

During the period of training children take an interest in their genitals and excrement. They are permitted to visually examine their urine and feces, are discouraged from touching them, but are not reprimanded for handling or visually examining their genitalia. When a child sitting on the potty is observed fondling his genitals, the mother may say, smiling, "What you doing?" The child responds with a smile and continues the activity.

A playful and entertaining attitude toward body contact is taken. For example, a two-year-old girl (Linda) was tormenting her eight-month-old cousin. The baby's mother, Joyce, reprimanded her verbally but Linda continued to punch and pull at the baby. Joyce got up, grabbed Linda, tickled her under the arms and fussed at her. The child laughed and let the baby alone. Joyce stopped tickling her, held her by the arm, and pinched her upper leg near her vulva several times. Linda stomped her feet and hollered. Finally, Linda's mother looked over and said, "Joyce, stop that. Linda, tell her to leave you alone." Joyce, laughing, released Linda. Linda, stomping her feet, said, "Stop it, Joyce, stop it." The sequence lasted about three minutes and illustrates one form that sensual stimulation takes. In many situations the child is permitted to explore and experiment with pleasurable body stimuli.

By the time children are toilet trained they have considerable freedom in the house and yard. When not interacting with adults, they are playing, sometimes under the supervision of older children. The young children often become tired during the day and nap in the midst of household activity or are carried sleeping into a bedroom. At night they share their mother's bed. They usually retire and arise together. At times the physical desire for sleep requires that their sleep patterns differ. The casual manner in which children's activities are organized and expressions of individuality are also evident in clothing styles.

Usually the children go barefoot at home year-round. Few clothes are worn during the warm months by any members of the household. Children usually wear pants and a shirt or at times girls wear dresses and underwear. Children usually select their own outfits and dress themselves. Their idiosyncratic choices of clothing are seldom questioned by adults as long as they are wearing an outfit that covers the buttocks and genitals. Children are encouraged to achieve independence in these areas and are not faulted for making decisions on their own.

Clothes worn at home are often in disrepair and a size or two too large. Neither parents nor children seem concerned. Since children are going to get dirty and probably damage clothing, there is little effort to maintain elaborate wardrobes. But every child has one or more complete outfits to be worn away from home which are kept immaculately clean and in excellent repair.

In all areas of childhood behavior a clear distinction between public and private behavior is made. Young children are permitted considerable latitude in behavior at home but when they are at church, shopping, or visiting they learn to behave and respond in a more structured way. Activities and responses are kept at a minimum and children stay very close to adults.

Situational behaviors are learned at about the time children learn to talk in short phrases. Most children learn to say "Mama," "Daddy," and the names of some family members before 15 months of age, and in time increase their vocabularies. Young children are praised for their verbal accomplishments and are stimulated by adults and siblings who mimic their verbalization and repeat words to them. The learning of language skills is interrelated with interpersonal relationships in the domestic group.

In their interactions and behaviors little children are obliquely praised for adult behaviors. Body contact and response to touch are very much a part of the childhood experience. Between one and three years of age, children's emulations of adult behaviors are enjoyed without reservation by all. When a baby responds to the music often playing in the homes, by moving his head and body up and down in time with the music, a great response is elicited. "Dance man," or "Dance girl, come on, do the chicken," is heard from the mother or young persons in the house. An older person will laughingly say, "Look at that, going to hell dancing before she can walk."

Behaviors which elicit adult attention and affection receive encouragement from adults. Little children are taught to go to adults with face uplifted for a kiss. A little later they are taught to hug and kiss adults, relatives, and friends. Teaching children to initiate affective interactions is repetitive. Children, particularly girls, are told to give "some sugar." In response, the adult hugs the child, kisses her, and often presses some pennies into her hand "for some candy." Soon the child learns to approach the adult and say, "Kiss?"

Between two and three years of age they become more practiced at imitating adult mannerisms. Little girls, particularly, learn to behave when dressed

*A little girl learns how to behave
when dressed up.*

up. They twist, smooth their clothing, and pat their hairdos. Boys disregard what is said to them and go off on their own more. Girls learn many of the mannerisms they see so often at home and these are remarked upon. When a little girl is told to do something she doesn't want to do, she tilts her face upward, casts her eyes downward, places her hand on her hip and puckers her lips. The position is very similar to that which adults assume when they are pointedly disregarding a speaker and presenting an uncommunicative posture. Little girls, dressed in new clothes with bows, colored rubber bands, and barrettes in their hair, look pretty. Adults, seeing them, ask to hold them, get "some sugar," and remark on their good looks. Most women agree that little girls are more fun than boys because they can be dressed more prettily. While boys also take pride in new clothes and respond to praise, little girls steal the show.

When children become practiced at emulating adult behaviors the response of household members changes. The comments to the child provide encouragement of their behavior but in a different way. Often compliments on a girl's or boy's appearance or behavior is countered by the mother, who states that the girl is "womanish," "fast," or "bad." To say that a child is "bad" is, in fact, the most commonly heard description of young children.[3] Between

---

[3] "Bad" has many connotations; some of them are very positive. For example, "Look at that bad car," means that the car is something special; it is the best. Similarly, children are all "bad" and expected to be "bad," but "bad" in a way adults respect or at least accept.

two and three years of age boys are usually referred to as "little men," are called "mannish," and are described as "hardheaded." Although hardheadedness is not restricted to boys, they are expected to "rip and run" more and to be less helpful in the home.

Discipline in the form of light taps on the hands or legs begins when children learn to walk. There are relatively few serious offenses for which the child is slapped or switched, although many women keep a switch handy to threaten children. The interaction pattern of adult and child relating to discipline situations follows a consistent pattern involving prolonged contact. The child initiates an action that is known to be forbidden. He looks toward the adult and the adult indicates with eye movements and a frown that the action is forbidden. The child draws back and then seconds later initiates the action again. The frown is repeated and a verbal rebuke added. The child pulls away, momentarily, and then begins again. The adult verbally chastises the child again. The adult's attention alternates between the child and other conversations or activities in the room. Ultimately the challenging interaction becomes unbalanced. When the child completes the action the mother promises punishment "the next time" and secures a switch with which to threaten him. The exchange often ends with the adult lightly slapping or switching the child. If the adult is anxious, angry, or disturbed about another situation not directly related to the child's activity, the punishment reflects her feelings. Children usually detect from the tone of an adult's voice and verbal reprimands early in the sequence whether completion of the activity will result in physical punishment. If the adult expresses sufficient anger at the beginning of the sequence, the child moves on to another activity before the adult is moved to action.

The testing of boundaries among young children provides them with frequent interactions and opportunities to explore their environment. Children are permitted considerable experimentation and are allowed to challenge the dominant position of the adults. In many cases, children are allowed to reverse the dominance hierarchy in situational events. The individual needs and desires of children are given expression in their behavior.

When children are between two and three years of age they have mastered many activities and mothers often describe with obvious pride how a little child can "do for himself." One young mother staying at home with her two-year-old and her sister's infant explained how the baby keeps her tied down. She feels that her daughter is "no trouble" because she can "pretty well take care of herself." When the mother wants to stay in bed in the morning the little girl gets out of bed, goes to the bathroom independently, and then to the kitchen to get her breakfast. She locates crackers or bread to eat and then turns on the television and watches it until her mother gets up. This child is similar in ability to other children of her age.

During the years between birth and three years of age children learn a great deal about themselves, those in the family, and public and private behavior. An environment filled with body contact provides many pleasurable experiences in sucking, eating, playing, and cuddling. Experimentation with the senses occurs regularly and is provided by all members of the family. Differentiation in expected behaviors of male and female children is expressed verbally by adults, in the behaviors of children in play, and in response to stimuli from adults. It appears that the basis for a high degree of personal independence, self-reliance, and individualism within a loosely structured and highly functional household is laid during the first three years.

CHILDHOOD

The characteristics identified in early childhood continue to develop but interactional changes occur in the family after the child reaches three years of age. A great reduction in interaction rates between adults and children occurs after the third year and continues throughout childhood. Greater independence of adults and greater amounts of time spent in children's play groups are notable changes. The importance of the "gang of older children" in the family is mentioned for children of about three years of age and older in another study among southern blacks (Young 1970:282).

An examination of the children's behaviors at about three years of age reveals a sudden change in interaction patterns when they become members of the play group. Children gain considerable independence of adults at this time. They usually retire and rise according to a schedule they regulate and rarely sleep during the day. Meals are usually prepared for them but if not, they are able to find fruit outdoors or snacks indoors to satisfy hunger. They dress themselves, unassisted in most cases, and select their own clothing. Older siblings or adult women usually comb their hair, a procedure that takes 15 minutes or more for girls but only a couple of minutes for boys. When young children need assistance an older sibling, cousin, or sometimes a young friend renders aid. The mother becomes the supervisor of play-group activities but close tactile relationships end. Children continue to be subordinate partners in the relationship with mothers but they escape outdoors and express their feelings and ideas freely in a children's play group.

Children's play groups usually form outside the house and are composed of children from two or more households. They spend most of the daylight hours outside and engage in a variety of activities. Running, playing in the sand, collecting ripe fruit and nuts, playing ball, and teasing one another are among their occupations. Play groups often venture into the house to request food, interact briefly with adults, tattle, or drift into indoor play. The presence of the play group in the house is short-lived. The noise, commotion, and confusion created by five or more children of this age are more than adults are willing to tolerate. As soon as the loud noise, pushing, and running start they are commanded to go outside. Sometimes they are slow to comply but the entire group is not permitted to remain indoors. In rainy weather, porches, bedrooms, and living rooms are the locations of play for one or more young household members, but the entire group does not stay in one house during bad weather.

Customarily, older siblings in the play group look out for the needs of the younger members. In later childhood girls become quite preoccupied with taking care of the young children. They are intensely interested in infants and babies and seize every opportunity to play, present them with toys, talk, feed, and hold them. These behaviors are a prelude to their own intense emotional involvement with child care in adolescence and adulthood. Their opportunities to handle and interact with infants are frequent but of fairly short duration because they are considered too inexperienced and rough with delicate

A play group poses with an infant kin group member.

babies. Despite their absorbing interest in babies they are relegated to the play group where they offer protection to the younger members there.

There are few rules governing the activities of the play group. As long as disturbances do not result in injury or come repeatedly to the attention of the mother, anything goes. Children play, share, horde, tussle, shout, and interact in a highly physical and verbal way. There are subtle differences between the behavior of boys and girls in the play group. Some of these are reinforced by the mother and others seem to develop unencouraged. Girls are expected to stay within the yards surrounding the houses, but boys are permitted a greater range and go into the thickets, briars, and woods which lie beyond the yard. Boys, who are considered rougher than girls, are not trusted with girls out of the hearing of the mother.

Older girls are more cooperative and protective of the little children and are encouraged to take care of them by their mothers. Girls are not permitted so far away from home in the play group but they are allowed to spend more time in the house. They are taught the fundamentals of cooking, cleaning, and child care through observation and example.

Boys are permitted greater freedom beyond the home. If they do not return to the house when they are expected (usually at dusk) no great concern is expressed. It is assumed that boys can take care of themselves and stay out of situations of conflict with older males or the law. Girls are expected to be in the house for the evening at an earlier hour and greater care is taken that they are not in dangerous company. Little girls, three and four years of age, are not permitted to venture from the yard to search for fruit with groups of boys. It is felt that the behavior of the boys is unpredictable and that mothers should not "take chances" with their daughters.

The learning of appropriate sex-role behavior is indirect. Girls about three years of age are taught not to sit with legs separated over the arms of a chair when wearing a dress. The instructions are not explicit as to purpose, nor are they consistently reinforced. The girl would not be instructed in the proper way to sit if she were wearing long pants. Gradually, the girl learns that she has both valuable and dangerous potential. Most mothers agree that girls have to be "watched closer" than boys.

Family members show little concern with modesty. During most of the year clothes are an inconvenient necessity and as few as possible are worn. Women are often at home in their bras, shorts unzipped, and barefoot. Males usually wear slacks and shirts or go bare-chested. The clothing of children is usually minimal. Most female children usually wear a shirt or dress while boys are usually bare-chested. In the home little about the adult human body is unknown to children although some private areas remain. Nearly all adults agree that some personal affairs should not be witnessed by children or explained to them. There is a taboo against children witnessing sexual intercourse. Children who share their mothers' beds are asleep when their parents have sexual relations, according to the parents. No child would dare question what might have transpired when they were supposed to be asleep. The patterns of communications are such that the personal affairs of adults are not questioned by children.

Children learn from about three years of age onward not to question the activities they observe at home. Their verbal communication is almost exclusively with other children except when requesting something from adults or being questioned by them. The restricted exchange of information between parent and child is transferred to interactions with other adults beyond the household. Children's verbal communication with one another is often intense and their vocabulary reflects their interests and activities. The patterns learned at home and in the play group are carried over into other situations, limiting the amount of information children disseminate about home. The communication pattern involving limited disclosure about personal behavior, parental activities, and household resources learned in childhood is refined in later years.

The experiences of childhood prepare children to participate in school, church activities, and other events independent of adult supervision. In early childhood and infancy adults cater to and interact intensely with children. Children represent personal accomplishments for parents and continuation of the descent group. The stress in childhood socialization on independence, self-reliance, and decision-making prepares children to become youths who can function beyond the home in a wide variety of situations.

CONCLUSIONS—PART TWO

In Part Two the role of kinship and family is examined through the kinship system, the organization of descent groups, households, and childhood socialization. The ambilateral kinship system permits affiliation through males or females and emphasizes residence as a determining factor in affiliation to descent groups. While there is a tendency to stress linkages through males, female links are reckoned sufficiently often to be a normal pattern. The importance of residence is seen in household membership and there is a tendency to reside with female linkages.

Women tend to prefer to live near kinswomen because it permits greater flexibility in household routines and the sharing of the maternal role. Household organization is loosely structured so that children usually live with more than one maternal figure and identify with the descent group they live with most often. The socialization process prepares children to assume roles in the flexible structure of descent groups and households and to develop relationships with nonkin.

When girls leave the play group for more mature behaviors, they become involved in household activities, all-girl peer groups, and in courtship. Their relationships in the household are altered and they develop various connections to community institutions. After a few years they usually become mothers, revitalizing the system with personnel and proving their womanly status. The process of family and community is elucidated in Part Three through the analysis of female maturation and motherhood.

PART THREE

Female
Adolescence—
A Rite
of Passage

   The discussion of socialization in Part Two ended with childhood, but
the process of female social and physical maturation is amplified in Part
Three. Here, the purpose is to analyze the behaviors, relationships, and events
occurring in adolescence and to describe the transition from girlhood to womanhood. Adolescence, related to biological change, is defined as "the transitional period between puberty (boyhood or girlhood) and adult stages of development" (Barnhart 1966:17). Adolescence is a transitional phase of social
ambiguity and disequilibrium in Edge Crossing. An examination of transitional states and their characteristics clarifies the analytical frame of reference
in Part Three.
   The most useful treatment of transitional states, for our purposes, is offered
by Van Gennep (1960) and Turner (1969) whose formulations provide a
framework to analyze situations involving ambiguous status. Van Gennep
(1960), writing in the first decade of this century, identified a common pattern observable in the various transitional phases in the life cycle. He termed
these "rites de passage," and described birth, puberty ceremonies, marriage,
fatherhood, pregnancy, childbirth, and death according to the pattern in each
of these transitions in diverse societies in the world.
   The periodic changes experienced through life are not only personal identity
crises, but events receiving recognition by society and its social groupings.
Van Gennep has shown that rites of passage are marked by three phases: separation, transition, and incorporation. Each of these phases is not equally well
marked in every ceremony, nor are the same rites equally elaborated in different societies. But transitions from one social status to another usually involve the three-phase process.
   Separation, the first phase, is comprised of symbolic behavior signifying the
detachment of the individual from an earlier status in the social structure,
from a set of biological or social conditions, or from both. During the inter-
vening phase, that of transition, the characteristics of the person are ambiguous; he passes through a cultural realm that has few or none of the attributes
of the past or coming state. In the third phase, incorporation, the person is in
a relatively stable state once more. He has rights and obligations to others of a
clearly defined or structural type; he is expected to behave in accordance with

certain expected norms and standards binding on persons of a particular social status in a given social system.

In some rites of passage a duplication of the three-phase process may be observed. Adolescence in Edge Crossing is a rite of passage with three additional transitions (pregnancy, childbirth, and the acceptance of motherhood) referred to here as subphases.

Turner (1969) has provided considerable insight into the relationships between transitional states and the social structure. Most definitions of social structure involve a hierarchical arrangement of positions, enduring groups, and adaptations in these through time. Another dimension of society is seen as community, bounded not by territory but expressed in the unity among those who identify with one another. In this conception of community, the designation "communitas" or "fellowship" is preferred to community because they differentiate it from more spatially bound definitions of society or community. Society, according to this conception, is relatively unstructured and undifferentiated and emphasizes the cooperation and communication of equal individuals who submit as a group to the authority of ritual elders. Communitas and fellowship are most recognizable during transitional periods.

Social life and the experience of those who pass through the social structure from birth to death involve successive experiences of communitas and structure, homogeneity and differentiation. The passage from one relatively stable state to another is through a limbo of statuslessness, ambiguity, and lack of structure. Each person's life contains periods alternating between structure and communitas, between status and role on the one hand and fellowship on the other.

In this study the primary interest is in one extended transitional phase, between childhood and adulthood among females. The institutions and division of labor, discussed in Chapters 1, 2, and 3, illustrate hierarchical arrangements of social structure. The discussion of ritual, where all segments of the community come together to renew bonds, reflects society in communitas or fellowship. The release from structure and return to it, in an altered position, effect adjustment to life crises. During transitional phases of life crisis events and other related conditions involving transition, low status, and communitas, persons share a common characteristic; they fall in the interstices of social structure, are on its margins, or occupy its lowest rung (Turner 1969:125). Females in adolescence undergo continual adjustment generally having each of the characteristics mentioned above during the process.

Female adolescents typically function in three areas: housekeeping within the home, courtship in the community, and in peer groups operating in both home and community. Their roles lack definition for they are neither children nor women, and they do not identify fully with any role. The ambiguity in their positions finds resolution when they become mothers, between two and ten years after the onset of adolescence. The processes of pregnancy, childbirth, and accepting motherhood are the three subphases in the rite of passage of adolescence. Girls are admitted to womanly status when they become the primary nurturant figures for their own infants. In Part Three, separation from childhood (seen in domestic responsibility), courtship, and peer groups are examined separately; courtship and peer-group activities are seen as closely interrelated.

8 / Separation from childhood

Outdoor play groups, self-reliance, and responsibility for self and younger play-group members were discussed in Chapter 7 as characteristic of preadolescents. In early adolescence, girls become involved in domestic activities effecting a separation from childhood. Responsibilities in the home, set events in peer groups, and pair events in courtship are interrelated experiences central to adolescent maturation. Their behaviors in the home are discussed in this chapter while in Chapters 9 and 10, respectively, courtship and peer groups are analyzed. Many events and experiences affect the maturation process; the discussion is ordered by the social and spatial realities of adolescent behavior.

Among girls the importance of the play group diminishes between 10 and 12 years of age, at about the same time secondary sexual characteristics develop. Initially, behavior changes are subtle, but when interactions within the play group diminish more time is spent in the house, assisting in household tasks, caring for babies, and attending to personal appearance. Young adolescent girls devote considerable time to their hair. They roll, straighten, brush, pick, plait, and dye their hair and experiment with coiffures. Hair grooming is a recently acquired skill because until the age of 10 or 12 their hair is combed and plaited by women without consideration to their desires. Clothing, selected in accordance with youthful styles, is altered to fit in ways they think becoming. Attention to clothing and hair styles and altered daily activity patterns are changes signaling the termination of girls' interactions in the play group. Girls are distinctive in dressing, grooming, and behavior from women, children, and men.

The self-reliance and responsibility in childhood become more pronounced in adolescence, contributing to strained relationships with adults. The interactions between a woman and her daughter follow a consistent pattern, in many ways similar to the pattern of discipline in early childhood. Adults usually assert their dominance over adolescent girls without physical punishment.

Although mother-daughter relationships are characteristically strained, it is in the home that girls learn housekeeping and child care, important for attaining womanhood. In childhood, girls are not permitted to be fully responsible for babies, but in adolescence they are encouraged to learn baby care through observation of other females and they are eager to be around children. Girls under 16 years of age do not usually have children of their own but eagerly seek out opportunities to interact with infants available at home or in related households. When girls are taking care of babies their charges are often mistaken for their own. Girls enjoy deceiving local residents and outsiders into

A capable adolescent.

thinking that they have one or more children when in reality they have none. Most adolescents are very comfortable with babies, have a repertoire of techniques for keeping them happy, and have a general knowledge of them. They make accurate observations about the needs of babies and easily establish rapport with them.

By the mid-teens girls have refined the ability to simultaneously talk on the telephone, feed an infant, direct older children outside, and prepare food. When there is a baby in the home and the mother works, it is the adolescent who cares for the baby and runs the household in her mother's absence. In some cases, the adult woman is the official baby sitter for a baby but her adolescent daughter is primarily responsible for his care. Girls attend school about six hours daily but spend much of their time with the babies and children under their direct supervision. Adolescents enjoy baby care, but often state that they do not like older children.

Babies are more pleasurable than older children for several reasons. They sleep a lot and cannot get into things. Girls can care for them while carrying on other activities. Care of a young baby permits intense, intimate interaction for fairly short periods. Older children demand less intense attention more frequently and often require discipline.[1] Perhaps one of the reasons girls do not prefer older children is that they are a reminder of the girls' recently abandoned childhood, while babies are associated with womanhood.

Adolescents demand and receive obedience from older children left in their care. Just as adults threaten to cut a switch to use on children, so do adoles-

[1] The diminished interest in older children is reflected in their participation in play groups at three years of age (see Chapter 7).

cents, but they are less reluctant to use them. They do not have the status of an adult and find it necessary to reaffirm their dominant position by force.

Girls run households very efficiently. They send children three years of age and older outdoors. Toddlers present difficulties but special treats like candy or soda and a free rein in the house usually keep them quiet. When older children are outside and the younger ones are quiet, the girls watch television, talk with friends, rest, eat, and listen to music. The also sweep the floors, dust, rearrange furniture, cook, wash dishes, do the laundry, and iron. Their performance at home is similar to that of mature women except that the household tasks are done less thoroughly. The role of adolescents as surrogate mothers establishes their claim to a limited female role away from play groups.

Girls' activities in the home are one dimension of adolescent behavior. There is an emphasis in early adolescence on domesticity, preparing them for adulthood. After they are established in housekeeping and baby care girls also become involved in courtship and peer-group activities. In the next two chapters courtship and peer groups, two closely interrelated dimensions of adolescent behavior, are analyzed.

9 / Courtship

The behavior of girls, separated from the play group but not yet fully involved in adolescent behavior, was discussed in the previous chapter. The rhythm of social behavior in courtship and peer groups illustrates the organization of adolescent social relations. Courtship, bringing together structurally different persons, involves series of pair events developing out of group activities where males and females come together expressing fellowship. Girls move out of the hierarchy of structure in family and community into courting situations. Courtship relationships are initiated at school activities, sports events, shops, and stores—in fact, wherever males and females meet.

In courting situations the expression of fellowship is the rule. Girls say that going to shops in the evening helps release tensions built up by structured relationships with adults at home and in the educational environment. The shop is physically and socially the antithesis of domestic life. The nocturnal activity in shops—the music, dancing, refreshments, and companionship of peers—all contribute to the ritual expression of communitas and fellowship. Shops, providing ample opportunity to meet and mingle with males, have an atmosphere accentuating feelings of unity and reducing the opposition between the sexes. Relief of tension, comradeship, and personal gratification are expressed as male-female sets pair off, ordering the prevailing egalitarian atmosphere.

Courtship relationships form between almost any male and female beyond childhood. Universal availability of males and females is assumed until otherwise informed but girls usually court males between their own age and 10 to 15 years their senior. Some categories of persons are usually less often involved in courtship; these include married women, persons in poor health, and the very old.

Among girls the stress of attending school and fulfilling household responsibilities builds up through the week. They feel frustrated and "held in" by the weekend and go to the shops and other evening events to experience release. Girls, dressing and behaving provocatively, dance, laugh, drink, and talk at the shop. On some occasions the group experience provides relief but at other times, when attractive males are available or they are involved with a particular male, the group expression of relief is insufficient and the physical need for sexual relations is experienced. Girls state that they feel like they will "go crazy" if they don't get out and "be with" someone. Girls feel that they "have it so hard" at home that when they get out they "let loose" completely. One girl developed headaches at least weekly unless she had sexual contact and usually experienced relief of a "headachy feeling" after having sexual relations. It is believed that sexual feelings are "human nature" and that they cannot be totally controlled. Physical activity, relieving emotional and physical tension, helps maintain equilibrium in social space. Tensions created in structured relationships are made more bearable by group expressions of release in shops and in courtship pair events.

Girls organize their courtship relationships to maximize their freedom. Their strategies permit them to remain attached to the family while experimenting with a variety of relationships. There is a tendency to maintain courtship relationships that hold potential for permanency, but the emphasis is on present activities, events, and pleasures. Females compare permanent, binding courtship relationships with their home situation. In each they feel that they are tied down and without sufficient freedom to behave as they feel. Most girls alternate between identification and support with the family and with males, achieving a degree of independence unavailable through total commitment to either. They enjoy freedom and are loath to be permanently or legally bound to a male when allegiance to their families offers them liberty and security.

Courtship patterns among adolescents reflect change and fluidity in partners. Girls tend to maintain courtship bonds with all males in whom they are actively interested. At times they number five or more interests but in other periods they court only one male. Married men are considered eligible for courtship but are often not preferred. Married men, girls say, can always go home to their wives when they argue with their girlfriends, while the single girls who court them "don't have no man at home." Girls are very reluctant to become attached to one male. They may "go with" one male and inform other interests of his primary importance but they do not completely sever their ties with other males. Diversity in partners is easily achieved when one or two of them live outside the community and probably contributes to the participation of nonresidents at shops in Edge Crossing. Many girls do have more than one courtship interest in the community and are successful in keeping boyfriends from learning of their other activities. However, the potential for courtship-related conflicts is high because jealousy is often created to induce males to behave more attentively. Girls usually manage their relationships without violence; they have numerous role models to follow in this endeavor. It is assumed, and understood by girls when they begin courtship, that few men are "contented" with one woman for very long. This contributes to the patterns of girls having multiple courtship relationships.

According to girls the practice of "special company"[1] is out of style because males would not keep up their end of the agreement. A male would request a girl's "company" and then not come to see her or take her anywhere. The girl, "stuck" at home waiting for him, was forbidden to go out and find companionship. Now, modern girls go out when they want, see whomever they like, and are not "tied down." The freedom to manage courtship independent of adult control provides girls with considerable individual freedom and a variety of options. The patterns associated with courtship events can best be illustrated through a case study. The involvements of one girl over a year's time are described below, followed by an interpretation of courtship behavior.

[1] See page 52.

THE COURTSHIP PROCESS—A CASE STUDY

Frankie Mae Wilson is an 18-year-old resident of Edge Crossing who graduated from high school in June. In January she was courting James, a man eight years her senior who had a "good" income.[2] James lived in a community six miles from Edge Crossing with his mother. He gave Frankie about $20 weekly and she thought of him as a good provider who could afford a home for her. Although she and James got along fairly well, he did not trust her and questioned her closely about her activities when he was away for a few days. She always assured him that "it be just the way you leave it," even though she was periodically seeing another man. James had many good qualities but Frankie was not "crazy" about him and felt that their sexual relationship left something to be desired. She was much more satisfied in sex and companionship with the other man, but he moved to Washington, D.C. in February.

Frankie was anxious to leave her grandmother's home because she was "dogged" (nagged) too much. In February she mounted a campaign to induce James to marry her. She pledged fidelity to him, satisfied him sexually whenever they were out, and frequently discussed with him how lovely life would be if they had their own place (and bed). James was not enthusiastic about marriage. Frankie sensed his feelings and altered her approach. She withheld sexual favors, saying that he did not "own" her. They fussed some but James remained noncommittal.[3] Withholding sex from James did not change his mind, but he did agree to marriage "sometime." He gave Frankie a ring, a band with five small stones embedded in it. This was tangible proof of his interests and they resumed sexual relations. Frankie continued to press him to marry. He said he wanted her to finish school. As April slipped into May, they had not made arrangements for a "place to stay" and Frankie became suspicious. She resorted to withholding sex and they eventually had an argument. Frankie threw the ring in his face and said that she did not want to see him anymore. There were a couple of brief reconciliations. James came to see her, gave her some money, and tried to reestablish his position, but she refused to be involved with him.

After graduation exercises she went to Orlando and visited her brother's girlfriend, Sue, for two weeks. She met William in a shop on Friday night through Sue. William, 19 years of age, was an entering college freshman and a football player. She and William were immediately attracted to one another and went out Saturday and Sunday night. She refused to have sexual relations with him on Saturday because she did not want him to think she was "too fast." But on Sunday night they went to X-rated movies. The movies excited her (she describes this as being unable to sit still, moving her legs together, and wanting to do what was on the screen). William's sexual prowess was delightful. They had intercourse five times and she did not get back to Sue's until dawn. Their relationship was very satisfactory sexually but was marred by the prospect of his leaving for college in August.

Frankie spent about half the summer in Orlando and half of it in Edge

---

[2] Girls feel that an income of $500 monthly is "good."

[3] Frankie said he was reluctant because he had a girl who had children "for him," but when he was gone once the girl went off with another man.

Crossing. William's talk about their living together after he was established in school pleased Frankie. But Frankie's mother and grandmother were not so impressed with William. They reasoned that he might get Frankie to support him while he was in school and then leave her for a woman with a college education after he finished. They were concerned because it would be years before he could help support her. Frankie was irritated about her family's interference but because she and William could not get established for several months she had to endure their comments.

Over the summer irregularities crept into the once dazzling relationship. William often preferred playing cards to going out with Frankie. In addition, Frankie suspected that he was involved with the mother of his baby, whom he maintained he no longer courted. Frankie, understanding his concern for his child, and unable to prove that he was involved with the woman, did not say anything to him about it.

After William left for college Frankie wrote him twice a week and received long letters from him regularly. Each wondered whether the other was keeping his promised fidelity to the other. Frankie did not court for nearly two months, honoring her pledge to William. She was experiencing mounting sexual frustration and felt that she needed to go out and enjoy herself. At work she met an attractive man, John, about 15 years older than she, separated from his wife, and a "sport."[4] He had "good" hair, light skin, was of medium build, and dressed "out of this world." John, Frankie reasoned, knew he could always "get his way with women" and she wanted to show him that all girls are not alike. But, when he grabbed her in the food storage area and kissed her long and hard, she felt she wanted to get to know him better.

John started calling her and coming by the house. Frankie, despite her interest and sexual frustration, was cool to him, told him that she was not like all the other girls, and restricted his contact to kisses and caresses. Frankie was enjoying the association. She teased John by telling him how "hot" she felt, dressed so that her best attributes were either revealed or closely outlined, and invited him over when no one was at home. John was increasingly anxious to have relations with her and was somewhat piqued at her reticence.

John was to come over on Thursday afternoon. Frankie finally decided that she would give him "what he want." She soaked in perfumed bath water, fixed her hair just so, applied her make-up carefully, dressed in a new outfit, and thought about how long it had been since she had been with anyone. John did not appear. Frankie was furious. In effect she had been beaten at her own game. She wanted to hold John at bay to show him that he was not as cool as he thought he was but she knew that if a girl holds out too long that the man will lose interest. When John called her the next day she acted mad and said she did not want to talk to him or see him. Eventually, he apologized for not seeing her and promised he would not do it again. In the course of the conversation she let him know what he had missed. He told her he would pick her up after work.

They went to his boss's house, where there was a refrigerator full of beer and a king size bed. Frankie told John that she had changed her mind and that she wanted him to take her back home. John persuaded her to stay and

---

[4] "Sports" are men with big, fast cars, expensive clothes, good looks, polite speech, and who use their eyes to express appreciation of feminine charms.

Frankie discovered why he thought he was so good. She said, "You heard that a small man carry a big load? Oh child, let me tell you, it be *true.*"

Eventually, Frankie told John about William and he agreed to leave her alone when William came home. John was agreeable to their just having a "good time" because he liked to play the field. In time Frankie came to like John both as a lover and a man. He did not seem so sure of himself and "sporty" as when they first met. She saw John every week and thought of the relationship as a convenient release for her sexual frustration.

Quite by chance Frankie met George, a carpenter, 28 years of age, from a community 75 miles from Edge Crossing. He was working in the development where Frankie's older sister lived. She and her younger sister met two men at the mailbox when they were visiting her older sister. Frankie was immediately taken by George. She and her sister went to the mobile home where the men stayed that evening. They talked, watched television, and drank. Frankie and George went into a bedroom "to talk" and eventually had sexual relations. When they were invited back the next night Frankie wore a lavender negligee and a trench coat. Frankie found George a fantastic lover, better than the others. She felt somewhat guilty about having sexual relations with him so soon after meeting him; it was something she had never done before. When Frankie told George about William he understood her situation. He was married and had children whom he loved dearly. He wanted to leave his wife but was afraid that she would not take care of the children.

During the first two months of their courtship Frankie and George saw one another all weekend bi-weekly. George had a number of "side hustles" complementing his regular income. He and Frankie traveled around the state visiting his family and lounging around pools at large motels. Frankie was impressed with George's generosity, kindness, and attachment to his children. Although she and George became close she was still committed to William. William returned to his home from college at Christmas time and Frankie spent the holidays at Sue's house. When she was with William she felt that they were made for one another. She was concerned that she had not been faithful but suspected that the same was true of him. Her suspicions were confirmed when she overheard William and Sue's father talking over a card game. William said that there were plenty of girls at college and that they could be visited in their dorm rooms. Frankie was not surprised that he had courted but was very angry when she confirmed that he maintained a relationship with his baby's mother. She said that it is not as good "to go with a man from away" from home because a girl does not "know his territory" and she cannot keep up with him. She also came to feel that William was taking more from her than he gave because she sent him money at college but he did not give her money even when he had it. She could not stand the thought of his spending her money on another woman and felt sure that he did.

Frankie went to Orlando less frequently after the holidays even though William did not return to college. George started talking about helping her with a "place to stay" and getting a car for her. Frankie appreciated George's qualities, including a solid income, seriously considered his offers, and backed away from her relationship with William. Her absence from Orlando caused William to talk in concrete terms about their future. He said he was going to New York to work and would take Frankie with him. They would live with his sister until they could get a place of their own. Frankie commented, "A man don't start tightening up on his end until you start loosening up on yours."

Eventually Frankie eased away from William, never telling him that she had found someone else. If George had not continued his attention she would have renewed her relationships with John and William. Frankie and George now live in University Town. He separated from his wife and Frankie broke off with John.

COURTING STRATEGY

Frankie's experiences reveal several patterns in courtship; girls court males for various reasons: affectional, sexual, and financial. There is an emphasis on courting males who have something to offer in terms of permanency, yet a reticence to be fully committed to one man. Most males are also reluctant to become committed, but when girls understand courtship strategy they evoke promises and behaviors from males. Withholding sex, jealousy, and reducing interactions were all employed by Frankie through the year. Frankie was careful not to terminate interactions with William until she was sure of George's sincerity. Girls usually have two or more relationships that can be reestablished when significant males become less attractive. Because males are often jealous of each other, girls use multiple-pair relationships to elicit more attentive behaviors from partners.

Girls tend to desire commitment from males and expect a measure of financial support from them. Girls and their kin are always on guard against males who permit females to finance them. There are males who permit women to support them, but most women demand that men pay at least their own way. Financial sharing among courting couples is expected but girls avoid males who do not assume financial responsibility and are not enthusiastic about males who do not freely offer assistance.

In addition to the more serious aspects of courtship, it can also be a game, as seen in Frankie's and John's relationship. Girls enjoy tempting and teasing males. They usually have a wide assortment of techniques to entice them and to satisfy them sexually, are proud of their expertise, and are always interested in learning more about men and sex. Frankie enjoyed both John and George because they taught her exciting and novel things to do sexually. All courtships have a strong element of play in them. One game courting couples play is to avoid sexual relations to see who "can hold out the longest." Females usually win the game and laughingly report that it proves that men cannot live very long without sex, or women. Gamesmanship in sex permits females to feel fundamentally important to males and for males to feel that they are irresistible to females even when women initially claim disinterest.

In courtship there is a tendency to use promises of fidelity as a means of strengthening bonds. Most males and females do not really expect to be faithful but do try to keep their primary partners from learning of other courtship pairs. Frankie did not ever tell William about her other involvements but she maintained the integrity of her relationship with William by telling the others about him. In the end, it was the jealousy she aroused in

George that affected his separation from his wife. Most girls accept males' interests in other females as a part of "human nature" and they, too, participate in diverse courtship experiences.

In most courtships, compatible personalities, financial arrangements, and sexual satisfaction are the binding forces. Most girls do not talk about "love." They speak about "being crazy" about a man, meaning that they cannot keep their mind off of him, feel that they want him permanently, and would "do anything" to "get him." Frankie was "crazy" about William but her "feelings changed" when she discovered George's potential. Girls tend to be "crazy" about males early in courtship days; later they have a more rational approach to courtship and its meaning.

Courtship is both gamesmanship and negotiation, reflecting pleasure, a measure of commitment, and the maintenance of simultaneous pair relationships. Courtship requires careful negotiations for girls to secure economic resources from males without becoming bound to them. Girls' relative independence and freedom is evident in the versatile and productive way they organize pair events. Reduced interactions in one courtship association do not terminate the relationship's potential for the future and do permit engaging in other courtship pairs.

Although it was not emphasized in this chapter, girls usually cooperate in courtship. They band together in peer groups to facilitate learning courtship rules and to meet males. Girls become involved in set events in peer groups and spin out into courtship. The process of group formation and peer-group activities are explored in Chapter 10.

10 / The peer group

In the last chapter courtship, a consuming interest of adolescents, was presented as a series of pair events developing out of group events in shops and other social activities. Girls operating in set events support their courtship endeavors. This chapter analyzes the peer-group behavior of girls in courtship.

Female groups of three or four members develop out of kin and friendship bonds. The nucleus of a peer group is usually the adolescent girls from related households, but kinship is not necessarily a requirement for membership. The girls maintain high rates of interaction, seeing one another or talking on the telephone daily. Peer groups do not have rigid boundaries but fluctuate as courtship and other interests draw members into the group. At any time there are about ten groups operating in the community tied together by members who slip periodically from group to group. Involvement in different peer groups is usually related to courtship. A girl moves into and interacts intensely with the peer group of a boyfriend's sisters while they court but interactions in that group are terminated when their courtship ceases.[1]

Membership in peer groups, most important in early adolescence, helps girls adjust to heterosexual relations. Usually the group's members are within three or four years of the same age. Membership in peer groups is necessarily fluid because maturation removes personnel from the group and younger members are admitted to membership. By the time girls leave school peer-group interactions diminish and some groups dissolve because there are no incoming members.

The entrance into an adolescent peer group usually coincides with the separation from the play group. The novice, recently drawn into the peer group, is guided in her pursuit of feminity[2] and males. The novice-veteran relationship is maintained for a period of a year or more. The novice gradually gains sufficient expertise in courtship and personal behavior that guidance is unnecessary. The sharing of knowledge and experiences becomes more important and intensifies the novice-veteran bonds. The examples that follow are set events illustrating the role of the peer group in facilitating male-female pairs.

[1] Males are not admitted to girls' peer groups although they often operate on the fringe of the group. These males, called "friend boys," assist girls in courtship but are never their sexual partners. They are structurally similar to brothers and are, in fact, related to some of the group's members.
[2] The novice-veteran relationship helps to ease the novice through menarche, techniques of feminine hygiene, and early sexual encounters.

NOVICE-VETERAN RELATIONSHIP

Courtship is organized around pair events, but peer-group members often influence the courtship behavior of girls. The novice-veteran relationship serves to educate the novice in courtship behaviors and includes an element of social control, as illustrated by the sequence below.

Three girls 18, 16, and 14 years of age are alone at the eldest girl's house. The two eldest girls, Marlene and Linda, sit at the kitchen table. Marlene's sister, the youngest of the three, is in the living room watching television and periodically entering the discussion. Her presence is not central to the events described here but she is a member of the group.

Marlene has a steady boyfriend with a good job and they are going to live together in University Town when she finds a job. Linda goes with a disabled Vietnam veteran named Bill who has a temporary cast on his leg from below the ankle to above the knee. Although Bill has a steady income and a nice car Linda is not satisfied with him because he doesn't come to see her often enough. She occasionally sees a married man, Joe, 20 years of age.

Marlene and Linda are talking about sexual satisfaction. They agree that all men are alike; they cannot be trusted but are good for some things. The conversation is lighthearted and there is a lot of laughter. Linda is considering breaking off her relationship with Bill because they have been "fussing" about his lack of attentiveness. The cast on his leg becomes the subject of discussion. Linda says that she hasn't been with Bill for over two weeks[3] but that when they "get together" she'll be "hot." She is joking about having to assume a female superior position when they have relations because of his cast and wonders whether relations will be satisfactory in an unusual position. Marlene assures her that he will be "hot" too, and will do anything to have relations. Marlene, laughing, stiffens her leg as if it were in a cast and moves about acting like Bill trying to gain access to his partner. Both girls laugh heartily and then Marlene says that Bill will really have to work to get Linda in that spot because Linda has been seeing Joe and will not be as "hot" as Bill. Linda denies Marlene's claim, saying that she and Joe have broken off. Marlene counters that she has seen his car at Linda's house. Marlene tells Linda she had better "watch out" because if Bill finds out about Joe, Linda will get "hurt." Marlene swings her fist through the air to indicate that Bill will slug her in the jaw with his fist. Linda insists that she is not seeing Joe. Marlene does not pursue the subject but states, "Well if the money's O.K. and the other's O.K. (meaning sex) you can't ask no more of a man."

Marlene assumes the role of the veteran by reassuring Linda that sex is fun whatever way it's done. Then, taking a sterner position, she takes Linda to task for going with Joe when Bill thinks he is the only one. The fact that Linda sees Joe is not so unusual except that she is only 16 years of age and Joe is married. Marlene knows that Bill has a very bad temper, and that problems often develop in courtship. Linda, by denying Marlene's allegation, indicates that she is ambivalent about courting the two men. In reality she would rather have a permanent arrangement with Joe, but he is married. Marlene, active as a supportive veteran in the first part of the sequence, warns Linda that her behavior is dangerous. Having brought the matter to light she lets it

---

[3] He has been in the hospital.

drop but adds a bit of advice revealing two important ingredients in courtship, money and sex. The sequence demonstrates the role of the veteran and
the influence she has in molding the relationships of younger peers. The girls
involved are older than usually found in novice-veteran relationships and this
probably explains why Linda is not particularly responsive to Marlene. The interaction also reflects social control, because Linda is not sure that someone
will not tell Bill about Joe. If she gets "hurt" others will not be as sympa-
thetic to her as they would be if she were innocent.

FLUCTUATING PEER-GROUP MEMBERSHIP

The renewal of peer-group ties for a particular purpose is illustrated below.
Peer-group membership is usually fluid, adapting to the courtship requirements of members. Jean, 17 years of age, courted George, 20 years of age,
two years ago and was actively involved in a peer group with George's two sisters and her own sister. The courtship was terminated when George became
involved with another girl. When his girlfriend became pregnant, they married and moved in with her parents. Now George is unhappy and sees Jean in-
termittently. Jean is still interested in George but her grandmother does not
approve of her going with a married man.

George received two tickets to a semiformal dance in University Town and
asked Jean to go with him about a month in advance. Jean eagerly accepted
but knew that her grandmother would not permit her to go if she knew Jean
was going with George. Jean renewed her contacts with George's sisters and
arranged to spend the weekend of the dance with them. George picked Jean
up from his mother's house and returned her there early the next morning.
George's mother works an evening shift and was unaware (but probably would
not have minded) that Jean had been out with George. While they were at the
dance George's sisters were at home and had planned a story in case Jean's
grandmother called.

Peer-group membership fluctuates, including members who can assist in
courtship and excluding those who do not need the support and assistance the
group offers. Jean had not been interacting with George's sisters, but when an
important event came up she was able to call on them for assistance. The
fluidity, based on courtship, is characteristic of peer groups. The social support girls give one another is also seen in their public behavior.

MEETING MALES—GROUP AND PAIR EVENTS

Joyce, 17 years of age, Debra, 16, and Terry, 18, are on a shopping excur-
sion in University Town. They laugh and visually examine "soul brothers"
they encounter. Each girl sees males she considers attractive and suggests
quietly that the others inspect them. As they move along the sidewalk they
attract attention, particularly from black males, because they are well-propor-
tioned, brightly dressed, and noisy. Usually they look at males without
"catching their eye" but often males say "Hello," or "How you?" and the girls
respond "All right."

The girls decide they will go to a cafeteria for a soda. Joyce suggests the

Males often attend to their appearance for courting.

location because a male she courts works there. She has not heard from him recently and wants to let him know she is around. The girls enter the cafeteria, looking around in every direction. They get their drinks and take a table. John, Joyce's interest, enters. Joyce looks away from him and the other girls burst into a peal of laughter. John, of course, notices them and comes over to the table. Debra and Terry continue to laugh, look from John to Joyce, and sip their sodas. John stands beside the table; Joyce avoids eye contact with him but they talk for two minutes. Then he states that he has to go back to work and leaves. Joyce sits dreamily sipping her soda while Debra and Terry look at the three other black males in the room, laugh and whisper, heads together. One of the males standing beside a cigarette machine catches Debra's eye and motions for her to come over. She goes over and they stand talking for about three minutes. When Debra comes back to the table she states "Shoot, we had us a conversation going there until he saw this," picking up a man's high school ring she is wearing around her neck. She is obviously disappointed at the turn of events, takes the ring off, puts it in her pocket, and says "Now, let me see what else there be." The girls spend 45 minutes in the cafeteria. John comes back to the table twice. He states to Joyce that he is going to Chicago in two weeks to work but that he will be seeing her. Joyce interprets his statement to mean that he is going to call her before he leaves.

Satisfied, the girls get up and leave. Their behavior illustrates their support in courtship endeavors. All of them actively look at males, make judgments about their attractiveness, but stop short of meeting men in the street. In slightly more structured situations, such as in the cafeteria, girls initiate action. Laughing, whispering, and looking, their own interactions elicit responses from males. Of course, they chose a particular cafeteria because Joyce wanted to see a particular male.

Joyce's quiet, reticent behavior in John's presence, contrasted with Terry's and Debra's giggling and laughter, indicated to John that their visit was no coincidence. Joyce's interpretation of his statements eventually proved accurate. He called her and they went out and had a "good time" before he left for Chicago.

Peer-group members consistently act on the behalf of other members and support their courtship behaviors. Girls in groups of three or four routinely go to the shops and other places of entertainment. Sometimes they meet attractive males but sometimes they return home together too. After girls are well integrated into courtship they require less social support and often go to evening entertainment with only one other girl, but females rarely go anywhere at night alone. Among younger girls more numerous companions more often result in the kind of activities they seek.

The behavior of adolescent girls involves activities in the home, peer-group events, and courtship. There is an emphasis on physical pleasure, escaping from the control of adults, and mingling with males and females in group situations, expressing the fellowship of equals. Courtship offers an escape from domesticity, yet a relationship with one male is too binding. Peer groups are structured to support girls in their maturation but are not permanent bonds. The ebb and flow of interactions in the home, courtship, and peer group express the ambiguous status of girls.

The resolution to indefinite status eventually is found in pregnancy. Sometimes pregnancy occurs before girls are integrated into the courtship pattern; for others it occurs at a fortuitous time, when they are involved with a male with whom they want to have a permanent association. Regardless of timing, pregnancy and childbirth and the acceptance of motherhood serve to alter girls' social relations and admit them to womanly status. This process is examined in the next three chapters.

11 / Pregnancy—one subphase

The transition from childhood to adulthood is a rite of passage with a long transitional phase. The transition is a period of learning the feminine role and lore, courtship, and household responsibility. In rites of passage where the transitional phase is elaborate and constitutes an independent state, as in adolescence, the arrangement of the three phases is reduplicated. The analysis of pregnancy, delivery, and acceptance of motherhood reveals a reduplication of the process seen in adolescence.

In pregnancy, and more dramatically in childbirth, the girl is dependent, helpless, held in suspense and dread only to be elevated to a higher status for having endured the process. Turner (1969:201) states that when liminality appears in rites of passage the neophyte is humbled precisely because he is to be structurally exalted at the end of the rites. Status elevation for females occurs some time after delivery in the post-liminal phase. Incorporation into adulthood occurs only after she demonstrates to the satisfaction of adult women that the process of pregnancy and childbirth have had their proper effect. Humbled by the discomforts and sacrifices required by childbirth, women deserving adult status assume full responsibility for their infants in relation to physical needs, and to the kin group.

With the pattern of rites of passage as a model, the processes of pregnancy and childbirth are examined. Then, the final rite of passage—acceptance into motherhood, admitting the female to adult status—is analyzed. The discussion focuses on girls who deliver infants surviving the first year of life. Adult status is achieved through procreation. Although education, employment, religious endeavors, and the care role can ultimately produce adult status without procreation they are less frequently seen in Edge Crossing. Through such endeavors adulthood is achieved much later and the transitional phase between childhood and adulthood is terminated more gradually.

Among adolescents who infrequently utilize birth control, pregnancy is not an unanticipated outcome of courtship. When pregnancy occurs it is often met with ambivalence because various social reationships necessarily undergo alteration and produce disequilibrium requiring unfamiliar interactions. Girls perceive that pregnancy can strengthen, formalize, and validate courtship bonds. Even though pregnancy may not be "planned" in the current usage of the term it is a fortuitous event with relatively predictable results.

Girls usually become pregnant in the middle or late teenage years, after they have acquired a body of female lore relating to courtship, feminine behavior, and sexuality. The first awareness of pregnancy usually marks interactional shifts in courtships, adult-adolescent interactions, and peer-group activities which become more obvious as the pregnancy develops. In the first trimester of pregnancy most girls divulge their condition to very few persons because these early months are uncertain ones. They are not positive that they are pregnant and have not become comfortable with the possibility. Cessation of menstruation is not regarded as a positive sign of pregnancy because they often have menstrual irregularities that include amenorrhea. Nausea, pica, and "brightening" of the skin are considered early symptoms of pregnancy. Breast enlargement, usually occurring in pregnancy, is not seriously regarded because many girls are still experiencing developmental growth at their first conception. The physical signs of early pregnancy are often easy to disregard. Sometimes girls feeling ambivalent about pregnancy pass the symptoms off and avoid serious consideration of the consequences until later.

When young women look back on their first pregnancy many of them recall that cessation of menstruation was a signal to them but that other symptoms were more important. Some girls "know" from the moment of conception that they are pregnant. One recalled that she got a "chill" after having sexual intercourse and a twitch in her eye later in the evening. The chill indicated that she was pregnant and the twitch in her eye was a sign of good luck. Some youths who "know" that they are pregnant minutes or hours after sexual relations say that they "just feel funny" in the region between the sternum and pubic bone and know that the feeling can mean only that they are pregnant.

While some girls are sure of pregnancy right from the start, others are unaware of their condition until they are told by someone else. Often it is through customary interactional sets that pregnancy is realized. Males have a special ability to detect pregnancy. It is sometimes a girl's sexual partner who tells her that she is pregnant. Because women "be more quarrelish" from the onset of pregnancy, some men know from a woman's attitude that she is pregnant. It is also said that a woman "feels different on the inside" during intercourse and men detect pregnancy in this way. Adult women in the household often keep a careful eye on girls despite a lack of verbal communication. When a girl experiences amenorrhea the adult asks, "How come I ain't seen nothing?" The girl responds, "You just ain't been paying attention, I been coming around." As time passes the facts inevitably become known, but girls are relatively successful in keeping pregnancy a secret until they are ready to cope with the alterations in social interactions it brings.

A girl's relations with her boyfriend necessarily undergo change as a result of pregnancy. For most, it is an event creating a bond of common interest between them for life. The pregnancy and forthcoming child symbolize a union between them of greater significance than courtship offered. Procreation is a serious matter; it brings together not only the prospective parents but their descent groups as well.

It is difficult for girls to anticipate how males will respond to their pregnancy. Most males are said to want children and feel "proud" when they know that they are the parent of an unborn child. Even so, the timing, their feeling for the expectant mother, or other courtship and family relationships may cause the event to be less than warmly welcomed.

Clearly, both males and females are aware that pregnancy is a distinct possibility in courtship, but males often respond in what females describe as unexpected ways. A girl aims toward eliciting from the male acknowledgement of paternity and symbolic or tangible evidence of continuing interest in his child and thereby the mother. Girls normally approach the subject of pregnancy before it occurs and have some idea of how the male feels about her "having a baby for him." After conception girls often do not tell the prospective father that they are pregnant. Their behavior, including pica and appetite and mood changes, is empirical evidence that eventually reveals to him that pregnancy has occurred. They may continue the relationship for three or four months while the male tells the girl that she is pregnant and she either denies or ignores his statements.

Even after the girl is sure that she is pregnant she may not openly admit it to the prospective father. Instead, she hints, remarks on how she feels and dodges his direct questions. The indirect approach to such matters is in consonance with the practice of keeping males in suspense.

When a girl is pregnant her status relative to all others is changed. Ideally, the prospective father becomes more solicitous of her. The usual reciprocity that flows between courting couples continues but the male increases his contribution because of "the baby." In early pregnancy both parties are cautious in requesting or providing further commitments. A girl usually reduces or terminates other courtship relationships while she is adjusting to pregnancy and formalizing her relationships with the baby's father and his family. Interactions in her household affect the approach a girl makes to the prospective father. If girls are "dogged" too much at home they tend to increase pressure on the father to "take care" of them, marry, or form a separate household. On the other hand, if the prospective father is too reticent in assisting her in the expected ways, her family supports her more actively and verbalizes disapproval of the male who "messed her up." The interrelations between the two are reciprocal and the girl is influenced in her decisions in one by the interactions in the other. Youths tend to achieve a balance between the two, but it is more often the girl's family that is primarily responsible for her support, especially during the first pregnancy.

Many girls and adult women state that a girl is entitled to one pregnancy before marriage but that she had better marry before the second child is born or risk being "put out" of the house. When girls have a first child they are socially not adults but usually have assumed adult roles when they become pregnant a second time. The stress placed on having a male support them after the first child expresses the responsibility adult women are expected to assume regarding their offspring. Despite adults' expectations of young women they do not usually insist that they leave home. The composition of households in the community indicates that few girls are "put out" even if they do not gain support of males after first pregnancies.

A closer examination of male-female relations during pregnancy clarifies why girls usually maintain strong ties with their families. Sometimes a girl is unsure who is the father of her unborn child, and certain problems ensue. It is considered foolish and slightly immoral for a girl to be uncertain about the paternity of her child, who will need to know his kin so that he will not unwittingly marry a relative. When the paternity of the unborn child is uncertain, the girl usually assigns a father to him; the male designated as father can accept or refute his involvement. It is said that a girl may be "liking one boy" and "going with" another. When she becomes pregnant she "puts it" on the one she likes and hopes he'll "do right by her." The alleged father may disclaim any involvement. In other cases, the father does not want to "settle down," so that the girl's most reasonable alternative is to remain with her own family. Sometimes the man has heard or believes that the young woman has been unfaithful and he refuses to accept responsibility for the pregnancy even though he, and everyone else, "knows" the baby is his. On rare occasions the girl refuses to divulge the identity of the father; he may be married to a local resident or related to her by blood or marriage. Pregnancy is one way that females gain adult status and achieve an identification with a descent group other than their own. These changes are sufficiently important that girls are willing to undergo the process even if there is no assurance that males will accept paternity.

The response of males is more unpredictable than that of adult women, who usually support and assist girls through their first experience in womanly endeavor. Adult women are verbally uncommunicative with girls about courtship but often make careful observation of their behavior, know when they are pregnant, and behave as if they are very displeased about the event. In early pregnancy girls are subjected to leveling to a low status position and are separated from their former status. They are accused of being "messed up" and of having behaved disgracefully. They are indicted for having "gotten the baby in the streets" and for persistently "laying up under some man." They may have thought they were "smart" but they will find out what all that "running" leads to when they have the baby and they will surely "pay" for all that fun. The girl is said to be personally responsible for bringing an innocent soul into the world who could have "stayed in heaven" where he belonged. The financial worries and other problems children bring are paraded in front of the girl and the most dramatic example of how troublesome children are is personified in the girl's pregnant condition. The tirades of adult women are frequent and merciless against girls suspected of being pregnant or who have recently been diagnosed as pregnant. Girls endure the abuse with downcast heads as if properly ashamed of their actions and of the result.

The initial displeasure of adult women toward a girl's pregnancy is anticipated. If the adult continues to "dog" her more than a month or so she becomes anxious to persuade the prospective father to help her escape the situation. This is rarely necessary because after the girl has been made to feel her low status and insecure position, the accusations subside.

Eventually the physical and emotional load the girl is carrying is acknowledged by adult women and they share with her their own experiences with pregnancy and childbirth. The support offered by adult women helps to "lighten the burden" she bears. She is relieved of some household tasks and permitted to sleep and rest as much as she needs. The sharing of experiences with women who have experienced pregnancy and childbirth draws the girl closer to them, helps her adjust to the process, and prepares her for childbirth. Remedies for common complaints of pregnancy, proper behavior, and other knowledge are transmitted to her. Many of the beliefs and practices she learns during pregnancy have been documented by Murphree (1968), who worked in a north-central Florida community but did not restrict her research to blacks.

Pregnancy demonstrates the power of the weak (Turner 1969) because in pregnancy girls are simultaneously separated from their former status and drawn into knowledge and behavior reserved for adults. The growth and continuity of the kin group is dependent on procreation so the pregnant girl contributes to the strength of the group. After pregnancy occurs, the prospective father is measured not as a fanciful boyfriend but as a potential family member. He is permitted more familiarity with the girl at home and spends more time in interactions with family members.

The girl's mother has an interest in formalizing the relationship between the prospective mother and father, but there is a strong reluctance by either party to act impulsively. While a few men deny paternity or refuse to support a child in some way, both males and females are reluctant to become legally bound in marriage.

Most women agree that girls should not be pushed into marriage or any permanent relationship if they are not ready or do not feel that they have found "the right man." It is better for a girl to have a child who is wholly dependent on her family than to force her into a relationship with a man with whom she is not happy. Loosely structured relationships in which the male acknowledges paternity and does "what he can" for the mother and her family seem to prevail. Often prospective parents do marry while the girl is pregnant, but there is little familial pressure for them to do so.

During pregnancy the male usually financially and emotionally supports his girlfriend as well as possible. He is drawn more closely into her home and establishes reciprocal relationships with her kin. One dimension of his behavior by which his potential is measured is the amount of time he spends with the pregnant girl and the lengths to which he goes to attend to her desires and needs. Many prospective fathers pay the hospital and physician's fees connected with the birth. The baby often carries the surname of his father even though his parents are not married. The father's behavior symbolizes his involvement in the procreative process and his claim to the offspring.

Girls often develop strong ties with the prospective father's female kin. In early pregnancy the paternal kin behave similarly to the girl's own kin. They deny their concern over the pregnancy and say that it is up to the girl and her mother to keep her "out of trouble." As the pregnancy progresses they demonstrate concern for her and are solicitous of her needs, share their pregnancy and childbirth experiences with her, and ask how "their" unborn baby is doing.

The more intense interactions of the girl with adult female kin, the prospective father, and his kin alter her interactions in the peer group. By the fifth month of pregnancy she withdraws from school, reducing even further her peer-group interactions. The important business of learning feminine lore about pregnancy, altering courtship relationships, and coping with the emotional and physical demands of pregnancy removes her from former entertainment activities. In addition she is separated from peers because she has gained an altered status. Former close friends think she is acting "grown" and "too smart" for them. The camaraderie of the peer group is never regained. Later, when other peers are also mothers, close friendships are renewed, but the sharing of activities, feelings, and experiences is not as open and the common adult enemy has vanished.

Pregnancy involves several novel interactional sets that reflect the altered status of the pregnant girl. Introduction to the health-care process during pregnancy usually occurs between the third and sixth month. Girls have little or no experience in the health-care system before pregnancy. They are prepared for the event by women who describe the process or are told that they will find out what it is like soon enough. They are always left with the impression that no matter how disturbing the initial examination is, it is nothing in comparison to the labor experience.

Girls are usually accompanied to prenatal visits by an adult woman who knows the clinic or office procedure. The adult takes care of all contact with health personnel up to the entry of the girl into the examining room. The adult provides support and guidance for her in securing care and in coping with the system, but during the most anxiety-provoking part of the process she is left unsupported. The girl enters the examining room in the presence of strange medical personnel, is stripped of her clothing, and offered a skimpy gown to cover her nakedness. She provides the answers to questions on her medical history with the meager information she has garnered about her own and her family's health. Then she is directed to lay on a narrow, hard table while she is quizzed, palpated, and examined verbally and physically. The pelvic exam, reserved for the end of the examination, is more threatening than the rest and it is often perceived as painful.

The girl endures the whole procedure with a minimum of comment and complaint. This is a moment in and out of time (Turner 1969); she is utterly separated from the normal social life, ground down to the lowest level, and deprived of the normal attributes of her status. The anxiety generated is great but she emerges more confident than before. All has been revealed and seemingly, nothing lost. The anxiety gives way to success and an off-handed attitude. In retrospect it was nothing in comparison to her expectations; having endured the process she is better equipped to cope with the trials and dangers that lie ahead in the path toward womanhood.

Girls become fairly well-adjusted to the fact of pregnancy and the alterations in interactions it produces by the seventh month. Having withdrawn from school, they spend their days at home, engaging in housework, talking with women, and courting. The expected behavior, practices, and beliefs associated with pregnancy have become part of their knowledge. The pregnancy, obvious to all, is publicly acknowledged and the courtship relationship is relatively stable. The prospective father "sits with" the girl at home rather than engaging in normal courtship behavior for fear that dancing, drinking, and excitement will harm the mother or the baby. Some girls express a desire to get out, dance, drink, and have sexual relations toward the end of pregnancy, but they are usually protected from these desires by solicitous females or the prospective father.

It is in the latter months of pregnancy that the suggestion of incorporation into the status of pregnancy is present. Girls spend most of their time resting, waiting, and sleeping. Their interactions in all sets diminish and they await the completion of the process. The physiology of pregnancy with strain on the various bodily systems explains some of their lethargy but the time spent in quiet reflection is something more. Having heard the lore of pregnancy and childbirth from others, they are vaguely anxious about childbirth, but it lies too far in the future to actively worry. The "fullness" they feel, backaches, constipation, leg cramps, and swelling in the feet are problems to be treated and endured.

Incorporation into the status of pregnancy is never complete because the patient waiting gives way to anxious anticipation of the baby's birth. Relief from the physical burden and desire to know whether the baby is male or female and healthy or not contribute to restlessness near term. Girls are caught in a double bind, wanting to be relieved of pregnancy but dreading the ordeal of childbirth. Most of them are ready to be through with pregnancy when they begin labor.

Before proceeding to a discussion of childbirth in Edge Crossing it is helpful to discuss the ideology of childbirth among middle-class Americans during the past 25 years. Dick-Read (1956) popularized the concept that knowledge about and relaxation during labor resulted in women experiencing less discomfort during birth. Dick-Read proposed that fear of pain during birth led to the muscular tension that caused pain; breathing exercises to enhance relaxation and prevent pain were described. Other volumes (Karmel 1959) based on similar principles but not claiming complete absence of pain during birth were introduced. Women using prepared childbirth principles during their own childbirth experiences formed organizations to disseminate childbirth information. Later, classes were organized throughout the United States to teach childbirth information and breathing techniques (Bing 1969).

The philosophy of prepared childbirth involves understanding and emotional support. Understanding the physiology of pregnancy, proper muscle preparation, and emotional support, primarily by the woman's mate, are stressed. During the past decade, prepared childbirth has gained great popularity among American women.

The participation of women's mates seems to be an extension of the family system of post World War II America. The middle class is mobile, separating women from their own mothers who traditionally assisted them during pregnancy. Shared conjugal roles in which male and female support and assist one another with most endeavors occurs. These characteristics contrast with male-female relationships in Edge Crossing, where there is customarily a separation of males and females in most activities.

There are probably very few middle-class women in the United States who have not heard of prepared childbirth. Most of them deal with pregnancy by learning about the physical and emotional aspects of the experience. Prepared childbirth classes are available in every major city in the United States and most smaller towns have organizations designed to assist women and men through their early parenting experiences. But it is largely the middle-class population which is attracted to the classes, suggesting that they are based on a strong middle-class orientation to parenting and childbirth.

Prepared childbirth classes and other materials available to the public suggest that sedation and anesthesia during labor and delivery are not necessarily beneficial to women and probably detrimental to infants. Many pregnant middle-class women seek the care of physicians who permit them some control over their labors and in the medications they receive. Hospitals are often described as unnatural locations for an uncomplicated birth (The Boston Women's Health Book Collective 1973). There is growing support for the availability of home delivery by parents who wish to avoid the hospital milieu (Lang 1972) and growing numbers of pregnant women seek the support of their friends and mates to assist them at home births. Relatively few physicians in the U.S. are warmly receptive to this extension of prepared childbirth principles and usually will not assist at a home birth or supervise midwives who wish to participate. There are, in fact, relatively few certified nurse-midwives in the U.S. to work in newly opening roles for them. A lay midwife lives in Edge Crossing. She is one of a diminishing number of women in the rural South who are not formally educated as nurse-midwives but are licensed by the state to deliver babies in areas where medical care is not readily accessible.

It is increasingly common for middle-class women to have sophisticated knowledge about their own bodies and to be prepared for the muscular contractions and discomforts of childbirth. They find childbirth a physically laborious and emotionally gratifying experience. Such women have different ideas and beliefs about the birth process, the responsibility of their mates, and the potential hazards of childbirth than do women in Edge Crossing. Middle-class women usually have children in their twenties, after they have had a variety of educational and employment experiences. In Edge Crossing, many girls experience their first pregnancy in adolescence, often before finishing high school or having employment experience.

To women in Edge Crossing, birth is painful and dangerous. They feel that it is proper for women to bring forth children, and for them to do so, as the Bible dictates, "in pain." The segregation of male and female roles in all areas of social life is redefined in childbirth. Women who have experienced childbirth are considered knowledgeable about it. Men are not expected to understand pregnancy and birth; it is not their responsibility to be actively involved in the process. Most women in Edge Crossing know women who have died in childbirth and all of them have known more than one infant who has died. In comparison, middle-class women tend to view pregnancy and birth as a normal part of their adult experience, and one without unusual danger to their lives. Statistically, low-income women die during childbirth and lose infants in their early years more frequently than do middle-income women. The experiences, values, and beliefs of middle-class women and women in Edge Crossing result in differing behaviors in childbirth. Chapter 12 describes childbirth among young women in Edge Crossing.

12 / Childbirth—a second subphase

The labor and delivery experience, second subphase in the rite of passage, differs in its social manifestations from pregnancy in many ways. The childbirth experience is of fairly short duration; socially it lasts a day or so and medically it is usually of shorter duration. Birth normally takes place in a health-care institution separated physically and socially from the community. Childbirth is a crisis for all concerned and is perceived as an intense, critical experience.

The enactment of the rite of passage associated with labor and delivery is discussed below. Before girls are ready to "get down" in labor they are treated more kindly than during earlier months. They are frequently asked, "How you feeling, honey?" by adult women who closely observe their behavior and reactions to detect the onset of labor. Usually girls are not sure exactly what signs are going to herald the beginning of labor but know that most women say that they will know when it happens. Most women consider the best indicator of labor to be the frequency and "sharpness" of labor pains. Usually expectant females have "little naggers" for days or weeks before the birth but when a woman is "really in labor them pains be eating her up."

The intensity of pain in labor and the way women "bear with" their pains is one aspect of labor all pregnant girls have heard about repeatedly. Adults often relate to girls their own experiences with birth. Most women say that they hurt very badly during labor but were determined not to make a sound. A few admit that they screamed, hollered, squirmed around in bed, and made "real fools" of themselves. The ideal behavior is to endure the "suffering" in silence and to pray to God for a safe delivery. There is little that anyone can do to relieve the pain of childbirth because it is a matter between them and God. In childbirth women are cast adrift from society and controlled by supernatural forces.

Girls, responding to the mandate to communicate with God, accept the "burden to bring forth fruit in pain" in a consistent fashion. They are very quiet about their expectations, the symptoms they experience, and about their own feelings. When contractions start they stoically endure them without comment and often do not report them to anyone because they may be told that they are not in labor. The onset of labor is usually recognized by other women who note behavioral changes in the girl, who may be up in the night to the bathroom or moodily changing position every few minutes. Adults question the girl to determine whether "it be her time." They want to know if she's "seen a sign" (the bloody, mucous discharge that often occurs in early labor) and whether her "water's broke" (amniotic sac has ruptured). Pains, the "sign," and water breaking are the three symptoms of labor most seriously considered by adult women. Of these, the pains are the most important because they ultimately push the baby "out of his bed."

Girls are not expected to be responsible for detecting the onset of labor, or for arrangements to get to the hospital. These are taken care of by adult women, who may recruit a man to drive. In the process of birth the role of males is minimal; the passage of the girl from pregnancy to biological motherhood is in the hands of women who know the process and its distinctive patterns. When it is decided by two or more females that the girl is in labor, a car is secured and she is assisted into it. Word is sent to the prospective father and a small cluster of critical personnel deliver her to the hospital. The prospective mother, the passenger in the process, is totally relieved of ordinary responsibility, interacting with no one, totally introspective, and coping with the involved physiological process taking place within her.

Socially separated from society, she is transported to an institution which removes her physically from the normal spatial, temporal, and interpersonal indicators of her status. The critical personnel accompany her to the door of the labor room, where she is whisked through a series of procedures designed to cleanse her of the physical remains of her former position. In the company of strangers, her clothes, hair curlers, and jewelry are removed. An enema and perineal shave cleanse her of impurities in the area of focus for the coming birth.

The phase of separation is clearly marked, and the break from the former position is abrupt. The short rite of passage of childbirth is indelibly etched on her mind. She can never return to the status of the uninitiated. The girl, utterly alone, stripped totally of her possessions, endures periodic contractions demanding her concentration. She is placed in bed in a small, sparsely furnished room and forbidden to get up; she calls on inner reserves of strength to sustain her.

After the initial, dramatic separation she is permitted minimal contact with social ties. She is allowed only one visitor because additional personnel increase the risk of contaminating the purified, ritual passenger with worldly pollutants. The visitor, her only link with previous life, and she have limited interactions because the contractions and physical process of labor require nearly all her attention.

The visitor, leaving the labor room regularly, reports to the critical personnel who wait outside the door. The number of waiting persons varies but the nucleus is those most closely involved in the girl's passage into adulthood. Most of them are female and include the mother, grandmother, sister, and prospective father. Those not physically in attendance are drawn into the process when they are telephoned and given reports on the girl's condition.

Analysis of the interactions and behaviors of personnel in the transitional phase reveals three distinct sets of persona. The focus of the ceremony is on the girl, who interacts minimally with the other two. The critical personnel who wait in the wings represent the skeletal structure of society awaiting the return of the ritual passenger in an altered status. The medical personnel are ritual specialists who supervise the birth process and assume total responsibility for her safe passage. Their interactions and expectations explicate their significance to the process.

The girl, relinquished by her family and friends, is socially in a limbo between life and death. Devoid of status, she endures the suffering she has known would be hers in the attainment of motherhood. She is neutral, dependent, unable to undertake the simplest tasks and barely in control of her physical activities. She is immediately dependent on unusually powerful strangers who perform complicated procedures and have medications mitigating her physical and emotional distress. In the limbo between life and death the girl is uncertain what is to be her fate. If continuing in pain is all there is to life she would rather be dead, yet death may be more dreadful still. The paradox of her predicament results in her joining the forces controlling her destiny. As the physical discomforts of labor increase she turns to the medical personnel and to God for relief and solace. Her cry, "Oh, nurse, help me, doctor, help me, Jesus, help me, Oh God, help me, please help me," is like a litany, each incantation pleading to a higher power to hear her case and have mercy. The drama acted out between the girl, medical personnel, and supernatural powers is divorced completely from ongoing social life.

The critical personnel outside the labor room wait, worry, and pray for a safe delivery or, if that is denied, her safe passage into the world beyond. Having only the power of prayer to influence the situation, they commit her to the hands of experts and to God. They seize every shred of information about the girl and examine it from every angle to evaluate its meaning. The wait, which may be an hour or so, seems endless. They too are drawn into limbo, humbled by the proportions of the crisis and immobilized until it is resolved.

Eventually the girl reaches the limit of her endurance. Fatigued by the force of the contractions and irritated by the length of the labor, she is discouraged because she may never escape the situation to live once more. She pleads for help and insists that she can do no more. She complains, "Somebody do something," surrendering any remnant of self-control. Agitation, discomfort, and loss of control noted by medical personnel are expected toward the end of the first stage of labor. The passenger, completely conquered by her physiology, has lost the measure of control she grasped so dearly. Simple instructions receive the response, "I can't do it." Medical personnel try to renew her courage, assist her with every move, demand nothing from her, and insist that she is enduring the worst, that she will "feel better soon." Unbelieving, the girl is sure she will never feel better and that the end is near.

Some women do experience a measure of relief as the cervix becomes fully dilated and the baby presses outward. The pushing response is a natural one but a medical professional usually stays with the girl, encourages, and supports her. Often anxiety and exhaustion allow no relief after full dilation and she continues to feel out of control until the birth.

The procedure of moving into the delivery room, positioning on the table, the examinations, and further cleansings contribute to further confusion and anxiety. The most frustrating and difficult part of labor lasts an hour or two but during this period the girl experiences the reality of possible death.

The moment of birth brings relief to her and the medical personnel responsible for her. She experiences immediate relief of discomfort and much of her anxiety. Within a minute or two she asks "What is it?" and is told "It's a boy," or "It's a girl. "Do you want to see?" The baby is held up, head down, cord cut and clamped, for visual examination. She smiles and is visibly pleased.

The girl, medical personnel, and supernatural forces have cooperated; she lives again and is proud of her accomplishment. She remains fully separated from the social world, her accomplishment unannounced to the persons who await news of her safe passage. Within half an hour after the crisis is past, the baby is transported to the nursery via the waiting room. Family and friends learn that the crisis is past by seeing the baby. The meeting is a brief one because medical personnel rarely linger long among contaminated outsiders. The critical personnel are pleased that their prayers have been answered and that the girl will be returned to them, elevated in status by her ordeal and successful completion of the test.

An hour or so after delivery the girl is transported to the recovery room, her condition still monitored by medical personnel. The visitor, expelled from the area during the delivery, is invited to return and they talk in subdued tones. She smiles and says that she is feeling fine. The visitor comments on the baby and asks whether she needs anything, but doesn't linger because medical personnel insist that the girl must rest. The visitor is satisfied that she is out of danger.

The interaction between the visitor and the mother is the initial sequence in the phase of incorporation into a new status. The incorporation phase occurs gradually as the physical condition of the mother approaches normal and she is integrated into the social behavior expected of mothers.

The interactions of mother and infant discussed in Chapter 8 are not repeated here; the focus is on the articulation of space, time, and the social realities of parturient women. The girl, considered out of danger when the delivery is past, is still in a delicate condition. Remaining in the hospital for two or three days after delivery she submits to the demands of the institution. Most of her time is spent in bed engaging in the procedures and routines required by medical personnel. She is presented with three meals each day, symbolically returning her to one aspect of normalcy. Regular interactions with her infant, scheduled between other routines, periodically remind her of the fruits of her efforts. She is permitted visitors at very restricted intervals so that her needs for rest, nutrition, and therapy are not interrupted by outside stimuli. The girl begins to realize the magnitude of her accomplishment by the behavior of the medical personnel and visitors. She has never received so much attention or been catered to so extensively.

Usually girls are presented with another indication of incorporation into adult society before release from the hospital. Medical personnel discuss with them their plans for future pregnancies and offer to provide them with the knowledge and techniques to accurately predict their next child. The panorama of birth control techniques are displayed and girls are permitted to choose, with minimal guidance, the most attractive alternative. Most of them prefer the contraceptive pill and are given a three-months supply to take home with them.

Most girls look back on their postpartum hospitalization experience as a "good time" with good food, "laying up in the bed," and few demands on them. But they develop a longing to return to social life. The critical personnel who delivered them to the institution return to recover them and the new addition to the descent group. The identical persons may not all return but appointed representatives are among them. The mother, her worldy possessions, and the baby are released by the institution and returned to society.

The girl returns home triumphant; everyone is impressed with the baby. She is required to remain in the house, keep warm, and wear shoes so that she does not get chilled and become sick. The baby is her major responsibility and she is forbidden to "stir around too much" for a week or so because it is thought to cause "female trouble," excessive postpartum bleeding and, later, loss of muscle tone. Other knowledge and lore associated with the puerperium is transmitted to her during this period. Engorgement of the breasts with milk is treated with applications of camphorated oil and by expression of the milk. Fish is avoided, as it is during all periods of uterine bleeding. A diet and medications encouraging regular evacuation of the bowels are administered. The girl is permitted to rest as much as necessary to regain her strength.

The childbirth process drains the youth physically and socially but she is restored to society in a different status. The baby and mother are as one. The baby, important in the continuation of society and in joining of two kin groups, is the substance of the mother's elevated position. The status elevation occurring when girls become mothers is dramatic after the humility of early pregnancy and childbirth. The father, visiting baby and mother as often as possible, sits with her and proudly holds the baby. The importance of the baby is demonstrated by the gifts, visits, and comments visitors make (see Chapter 7).

After a week or so girls are not considered so delicate and are permitted outdoors. They begin to assume some household responsibility and permit the baby to be held and fed by others. It is after the mother has regained her strength and is permitted to leave the house that she becomes involved in the final rite of passage between childhood and adulthood. This rite, enacted wholly within the social context, is less dramatic than that of childbirth, but is ultimately more significant. It permits the girl to choose between adulthood demonstrated by motherhood, or a return to adolescent behaviors.

Most girls choose the role of motherhood and adult roles without equivocation. The importance of the baby to the descent group is demonstrated by the vigilance of adult women. They do not permit the infant to be neglected. If the biological mother does not conform to their expectations she is relieved of the responsibility for her baby. All young mothers are observed for behaviors indicating a lack of interest in the baby and omissions are brought to their attention. The acceptance or rejection of motherhood is determined by the biological mother and women in the descent group. This process constitutes the final subphase into the rite of passage between childhood and adulthood.

13 / Assuming the role of mother—
a third subphase

The social process of pregnancy and childbirth, discussed in Chapters 11 and 12, reveals dramatic alterations in social interactions. In the third subphase of the rite of passage in adolescence the alterations in interactions and status change are less clearly marked but reflect the meaning of the womanly role in family and community.

Young mothers, after childbirth, are returned to the family and community in structural positions differing from those of adolescence. As mothers, their contribution to the descent group is recognized and they are expected to take a more active role in the descent group. It is through their behavior with the infant, females in the kin group, and in courtship that the role of mother is validated or rejected. Descent-group heads and older female relatives ultimately determine whether young mothers are admitted to adult status. Those accepting motherhood receive direction from their mothers and older women, share housekeeping responsibilities, and maintain relationships with their baby's relatives.

The close physical and emotional relationship of the mother and infant, discussed in Chapter 7, is one aspect of motherhood. The infant sleeps with the mother and she feeds him, keeps him clean and satisfied, and permits him to relate with others in the household. Consistent attention to babies' needs are expected of mothers, and are necessary for the mother's acceptance by older women as an adult.

Older women are generous with advice about baby care and young mothers are expected to listen to and heed it. Some limits are placed on the amount of time young mothers spend away from the home because older women believe that mothers should demonstrate their interest in their infants by attending to them consistently. The advice of older women and the requirements they place on young mothers reveals that they are leaders in the group. They serve to guide young women in motherhood and are responsible for the caliber of child care in the group. Young women acknowledge their position and care for their infants in ways acceptable to mature women. Although older women and young ones are not equals, there is reduction in the hostility that was present during adolescence.

Older women remain in control of household affairs but young women participate more actively in the decision-making and sharing of responsibility. Young women share in the care of other children in the household, keep house, and talk freely with women about feminine topics taboo in adolescence. Often, the sharing of household duties involves the young mother's staying at home with sisters' or mother's children while they work. Although these responsibilities are a part of adolescent roles, after motherhood they take on new meaning. The welfare of the mother and her child is tied more closely to the well-being of the group. Young mothers assist other women with their children so they can receive child-care services when they are out. Among women, discussions of child care and sharing of responsibility tend to replace peer-group activities of adolescence.

Young mothers maintain ties with their babies' fathers' relatives to establish infants' positions in paternal descent groups. Young women's position in paternal descent groups is through their babies and is expressed in attention shown infants and young children by their relatives. Mothers receive praise for babies' growth, good looks, appetite, and pleasant disposition. The relationship with babies' fathers' descent groups parallels their position in their own group except that the ties are less binding. Young women interact with their babies' fathers' sisters, sharing baby stories and occasionally child care. Babies are encouraged to go to the arms of "Auntie" and are permitted to crawl and play with their cousins.

Young women relate to their babies' paternal grandmothers as descent group heads. They receive favors and gifts from paternal groups but take care that their babies are not removed from maternal groups. For example, Rose, returning to school after having her baby, needed to find a baby-sitter. Her grandmother took care of a sick brother during the day and her mother worked. Rose maintained a relationship with the paternal grandmother who lived in University Town and she offered to take the baby for Rose until she finished school. Both Rose and her grandmother were polite but firm in refusing the offer. Rose said she wanted to be near her baby because he was her responsibility. Rose's grandmother did not want the baby "under" another woman when she could not be sure how he was being treated. Their responses reflect the importance of the baby to Rose in attaining adulthood and to the descent group. Rose needed to be in daily contact with the baby to validate her womanly status and her grandmother did not want to risk losing the baby from the group. They did want to ensure the baby's support from and identification with the paternal descent group. When the paternal grandmother wanted to see the baby, Rose took the baby to her house for the day and she and the baby sometimes spent the weekend with the baby's grandmother. Usually, Rose did not permit the baby to remain in the paternal household unless she was present.

Most young mothers recognize the responsibility they have to the descent group and to their babies. The role of mother requires many adaptations in their behavior, including courtship activities. Young women establish a permanent bond with their babies' descent group and usually maintain relationships with the fathers too. Although the mother and father may have other courtship interests, their involvement with one another through the baby remains. The sexual component of the relationship can be restored whenever it is mutually agreeable. Women who have children fathered by different men increase the number of courting pairs they can maintain. Although the potential for courtship is increased by motherhood, young women have to consider their children and the expectations of older women. The need for child care when they court draws related young women together. The pattern of young women courting after they are mothers is one point of contention with older women. They acknowledge the need of younger women to go out but require they do not court as extensively as in adolescence.

When girls are more interested in courtship, employment, or education than they are in their children and descent group, they often relinquish their claim on their children and return to adolescent roles. It is usually courtship interests that lead to children gaining new mothering figures. For example, Julia, 17 years of age, had a six-month-old baby when she went to Miami, Florida alone to stay with her aunt for a week. While there she started courting a man and did not return to Edge Crossing for three weeks. When she came back she stated that she and the baby were going back to Miami to stay. This plan was vetoed by her mother and grandmother, who said that she was not going to drag the baby "all over" (in bus stations, out at night, and around strangers) because it would make him sick. If she wanted "to be all the time in the streets" and had to get "the roaming out of her blood" that was one thing, but she was not going to endanger the baby. Julia protested, saying that the baby was hers, she "birthed him," took care of him, and she would do as she pleased. Her mother countered her statements by saying that if Julia took the baby with her, she would get "the man" (the police) to come get her and the baby.

Julia did not think her mother would really do that but the threat was sufficient. She went to Miami alone and spent about half her time there for three months. While she was gone there was considerable talk about her behavior. Her grandmother said that Nellie, Julia's older sister, was more like a mother to the baby than Julia and that if Julia did not care "no more about the baby than that" (going off to court) she should not be a mother. Eventually she returned to the baby and reestablished her claim to motherhood. In this case there was no woman immediately available who wanted the baby for her own, but if Nellie or her mother or grandmother had wanted to become mother of the baby Julia probably would have been encouraged to give the baby to her.

It is not unusual for young women to "give" their babies to other mothering figures at the urging of older women. Usually "new" mothering figures are related to the babies and are often their grandmothers or great-grandmothers. Women who are given babies, other than those in direct ascending lines, have few or no children, or have grown offspring (an example of this was mentioned in Chapter 6). Women who want to receive babies "beg" the mothers and older females in the households for the babies. They buy clothes and food for them, visit, inquire about them, and demonstrate their love and ability to care for them. When the biological mothers are not behaving in ways acceptable to adult women, the adults eventually support the desires of "new" mothers, pointing out the advantages of the arrangement to the biological mothers. Young mothers are reluctant to relinquish their children but older women persuade them to do so when other women demonstrate love, affection, and the financial ability to provide for them. When babies are given away it permits the biological mothers to return to courtship and other activities of adolescence. Mothers rarely lose contact with their children even when they leave the community.

One of the reasons that young mothers release their children is that they are emotionally involved with a man but estranged from him. They leave the community to forget him and are unable to take the baby along. For example, Gwen, 18 years of age, would not marry her boyfriend when she became pregnant or after the birth of her daughter. He pleaded with her to marry and was capable of supporting her. Gwen enjoyed the attention he showered on her and her baby but she had "turned against him" after becoming pregnant. Al-

A young woman with her children.

though she was "crazy" about him she "wouldn't have nothing to do with him" (sexually). Finally, when Gwen's baby was four months of age, the father moved in with a girlfriend about one-fourth of a mile from Gwen's mother's house. Gwen was "so outdone" that she wanted to get away from Edge Crossing and planned to live in Palm Beach with a cousin and work. Gwen's mother persuaded her to "give" the baby to her before she left. Gwen comes home to see the child, now two years of age, every month or so, but her mother takes care of the child and buys her clothing. The child calls her grandmother "Mama," and her biological mother "Gwen."

Giving one's child to a mother or grandmother is not as final or drastic as giving a baby to another relative, but the results are the same. Instead of taking an active role in descent group matters, the girl is returned to the activities of adolescence. The rite of passage of adolescence does not end abruptly because the acceptance or rejection of motherhood is a gradual process. The facility with which children change residence in later childhood is an extension of the process described here. However, when children change residence in later life, the claim of the biological mother to adult status is not questioned.

The tendency of descent group heads to hold children in the group allows girls and young women flexibility. They may court and live beyond Edge Crossing for extended periods without having adult responsibilities in the descent group. Girls forfeit the status of motherhood and give their babies to other mothering figures to regain the freedom of adolescence. Most young women enthusiastically accept motherhood and the contingent descent group responsibility. The acceptance of motherhood is the first step toward becoming the head of the descent group and to having a household of one's own.

CONCLUSIONS—PART THREE

The social maturation of girls from childhood until incorporation into adulthood was examined in Part Three. Girls move from play groups into positions of ambiguous status as they participate in courtship and peer-group activities. The responsibilities of girls in housekeeping and child care reveal their identities in the family and descent group.

Girls constrained by adults find release in peer groups and courtship. They share feelings and experiences with other girls and establish pair bonds with males, setting them apart from household obligations. In courtship, they employ various strategies to achieve bonds distinct from family and to communicate with peers, rather than adult women. Vacillating between identification with family and courtship pairs, their transitional status is clear.

Eventually, their position gains definition when they become pregnant. During pregnancy they become separated from extensive courtship, reduce peer-group activities, and align with adult women who instruct them in the lore of pregnancy and birth.

Adolescence and pregnancy follow the schema of rites of passage (Van Gennep 1960) but in childbirth the process is most dramatically revealed. The girls, removed from the community and family, are placed in the hands of specialists who coach and assist them through the process. Childbirth, an event linked with death, is a shocking and frightening experience, but following it girls experience a dramatic reversal in status. The humiliation and fear accompanying childbirth gives way to status elevation in motherhood.

When girls do not assume the role of mother, the descent group is equipped to support the children and provide mothers for them. A return to adolescence temporarily forfeits the girl's claim to womanhood and reflects the seriousness of the mothering role in the community.

Children born into descent groups are never left without mothering figures because the sharing of maternal role assures that one or more women will take them as their own. Girls usually accept motherhood and the authority of older women, and support the hierarchy in the kinship system and community. They ultimately become women who supervise their own children and accrue status based on the descent group they lead.

In adolescence girls are permitted latitude in their behavior. They are neither forced to marry nor to accept responsibility for their children. The emphasis on individualism and emotional expression seen in childhood, courtship, ritual activities, and household patterns is also given expression in the rites of passage of adolescence and the three subphases of pregnancy, childbirth, and motherhood.

Summary and conclusions

The modified community study approach utilized in this presentation permits the articulation of the material on adolescent maturation with the social, structural, and ethnographic features of the community. Community is viewed as having two sexes and three generations organized around spatial, temporal regularities of social life. Within the community one of the primary organizing principles is that of the division of labor between the sexes. The sexual segregation found in day-to-day life is redefined in ritual where males and females are brought together. In all community rituals, including sports, shop activities, and religion, the dominant role of males is expressed. Male and public behavior of blacks has been studied more extensively than other areas and some of the themes in the research results are seen here. The verbal facility of males, the importance of male gathering points beyond the home, music, dance, and games are seen in Abrahams (1964, 1970), Hannerz (1969), Haralambos (1970), Kochman (1970), and Liebow (1967).

In homes and in kinship there is a tendency for females to maintain strong positions. The kinship system, allowing land title and descent group membership through females, gives formal expression to the primacy of females in householding and child care. The relatively strong position of women in family and household are presented in other studies of New World blacks (Gonzalez 1969; Smith 1956). Black women are also described as forming relationships based on sharing of services and meager resources in an urban ghetto (Stack 1974). Earlier studies of blacks in the rural South also indicate that women have had an active role within the household and in child rearing (Johnson 1941; Powdermaker 1939). In Edge Crossing there is an ambilateral optative descent system. Whether such a model is applicable to other New World black populations is a question that may be answered by further research.

Descent groups and households permit children to be born and reared in a loosely organized household and to form relationships with kinsmen of various ages. The segregation of similarly aged persons within the kinship structure encourages strong bonds between siblings and cousins. The importance of the play group to youngsters, described in this study, is also discussed by Young (1970), who studied childhood in a small Georgia town. Children know a number of male and female adults from whom they learn expected forms of behavior. Although the system is flexible, there is structure. Children are conscious of their kin linkages and have affectional ties to many of them.

Children move beyond kinship relationships into the community (expressing in another way spatial and temporal rhythms) during the maturational process. Girls involved in courtship and peer groups have strained relationships with adult kin, who tend to protect them from the realities of the heterosexual world. Girls engage in activities in shops, where an egalitarian atmosphere prevails, and spin out into courting pairs. Shops and courtship are something apart from the normal social forms around which community revolves. Kin ties are not lost in adolescence but loosened to accommodate expanded social roles.

Adolescence is seen as a rite of passage in which girls are separated from childhood attachments and permitted to explore more mature behaviors. Adolescent behavior is necessarily a period of testing and experimentation because it precedes the adult roles in the social structure. In Edge Crossing girls are groomed more consistently for the maternal role than any other. In childhood they gain self-reliance and self-assurance in female endeavor. They are comfortable with sexuality and their capacity to be mothers in early adolescence. The natural culmination of femininity found in motherhood is not an unexpected result of courtship. Although girls are not taught the process of pregnancy and childbirth they are considered a natural consequence of maturation. Girls' lack of knowledge and apprehension in pregnancy serve to make the elevated status of motherhood more dramatic. The attitudes toward and knowledge about childbearing among rural black women provide a dramatic contrast with middle-class women, who seek information and beliefs sanctioned by the health-care and educational institutions of the wider society.

In Edge Crossing motherhood ties girls back into the social structure in an elevated status and provides for them the basic elements necessary to become leaders in family and community in later years. Womanhood is achieved through procreation more frequently than in any other way. This study questions whether other avenues of achievement, by education or employment, will become more important in expressing adulthood. At this time occupational and educational opportunities are fairly restricted, both by the wider society and by socialization in the home and community. Changes relating to the social expression of adulthood may be a topic for future inquiry.

Van Gennep's (1960) model permits an analysis of the social process of adolescent female maturation involving pregnancy and childbirth. This research indicates that the social process in rites of passage effectively prepares girls for the role of motherhood. One popular publication (Guffy 1972) captures the essence of female sexuality and motherhood for a black woman in the United States, although the background is neither southern nor rural. Guffy reveals, in part, the marriage system, one aspect of this study.

The patterns associated with adolescent courtship and which extend through adulthood reflect that marriage, as a lifelong, monogamous arrangement, is not usually experienced by women in Edge Crossing. The significant aspects of courtship and of marriage are financial support, sexual gratification, and children. Courting relationships provide the basis for male-female interactions. Most men and women do eventually marry, but often not until children are born and even then courtship behaviors do not usually cease. Courtship relationships are validated by births; the kinship system and household members provide support and structure for children in their early years.

The highly developed courtship pattern, emphasizing mutual attractiveness and pleasure, is an expression of the fundamental importance of sexuality. In Edge Crossing adolescent sexuality is acceptable and is expressed in courtship.

The human need for sexual expression has long been accepted as basic to human society and is, in fact, necessary for its continuation. This research suggests that the acceptance of and relaxed attitude toward sexuality contributes to the independence of women in forming courtship pairs.

Motherhood, in adolescence, validates adult status. In adulthood, children provide women with the potential to lead descent groups, to serve as a node for redistribution of resources, and to guide younger members of the descent groups. Motherhood is an important maturational event and, in maturity, provides women with elevated status in the descent group and community.

Bibliography

Abrahams, Roger D., 1964, *Deep Down in the Jungle . . . Negro Narrative Folklore from the Streets of Philadelphia*. Hatboro, Pa.: Folklore Associates.

————, 1970, *Positively Black*. Englewood Cliffs, N. J.: Prentice-Hall.

Arensberg, Conrad M. and Solon T. Kimball, 1965, *Culture and Community*. New York: Harcourt.

Aschenbrenner, Joyce, 1975, *Lifelines: Black Families in Chicago*. New York: Holt, Rinehart and Winston.

Barnhart, C. L. (ed.), 1966, *The American College Dictionary*. New York: Random House.

Billingsley, Andrew, 1968, *Black Families in White America*. Englewood Cliffs, N. J.: Prentice-Hall.

Bing, Elisabeth, 1969, *Six Practical Lessons for an Easier Childbirth*. New York: Bantam.

Brown, Claude, 1965, *Manchild in the Promised Land*. New York: New American Library.

Carmichael, Stokely and Charles V. Hamilton, 1967, *Black Power: The Politics of Liberation in America*. New York: Vintage.

Chapple, Eliot D. and Carleton S. Coon, 1942, *Principles of Anthropology*. New York: Henry Holt and Company.

Cleaver, Eldridge, 1968, *Soul on Ice*. New York: Dell.

Davis, Allison and John Dollard, 1940, *Children of Bondage*. New York: American Council on Education.

Davis, Allison, *et al.*, 1941, *Deep South: A Social Anthropological Study of Caste and Class*. Chicago: University of Chicago Press.

Dick-Read, Grantly, 1956, *The Natural Childbirth Primer*. New York: Harper & Row.

Dollard, John, 1937, *Caste and Class in a Southern Town*. New Haven, Conn.: Yale University Press.

Firth, Raymond, 1957, "A Note on Descent Groups in Polynesia," *Man,* 57:4–8.

Florida, 1970, *Florida Vital Statistics*. Jacksonville, Fla.: Department of Health and Rehabilitative Services.

————, 1974, *Florida Vital Statistics*. Jacksonville, Fla.: Department of Health and Rehabilitative Services.

Fox, Robin, 1967, *Kinship and Marriage*. Baltimore, Md.: Penguin.

Frazier, E. Franklin, 1932, *The Negro Family in Chicago*. Chicago: University of Chicago Press.

————, 1939, *The Negro Family in the United States*. Chicago: University of Chicago Press.

————, 1949, *The Negro in the United States*. New York: Macmillan.

Glazer, Nathan and Daniel P. Moynihan, 1963, *Beyond the Melting Pot*. Cambridge, Mass.: The M.I.T. Press.

Gonzalez, Nancie L., 1965, "The Consanguineal Household and Matrifocality," *American Anthropologist*, 67:1541–49.

————, 1969, *Migration and Modernization: Adaptive Reorganization in the Black Carib Household*. Seattle: University of Washington Press.

Grier, William H. and Price M. Cobbs, 1968, *Black Rage*. New York: Bantam.

Guffy, Ossie, 1972, *Ossie: The Autobiography of a Black Woman*. New York: Bantam.

Hannerz, Ulf, 1969, *Soulside Inquiries into Ghetto Culture and Community*. New York: Columbia University Press.

————, 1970, "What Ghetto Males Are Like: Another Look," in *Afro-American Anthropology: Contemporary Perspectives*, Norman E. Whitten, Jr. and John F. Szwed, eds., pp. 313–327. New York: Free Press.

Haralambos, Michael, 1970, "Soul Music and Blues: Their Meaning and Relevance in Northern United States Black Ghettos," in *Afro-American Antropology: Contemporary Perspectives*, Norman E. Whitten, Jr. and John F. Szwed, eds., pp. 367–384. New York: Free Press.

Herskovits, Melville J., 1930, "The Negro in the New World: The Statement of a Problem," *American Anthropologist*, 32:145–55.

————, 1941, *The Myth of the Negro Past*. New York: Harper & Row.

Johnson, Charles S., 1934, *Shadow of the Plantation*. Chicago: University of Chicago Press.

————, 1941, *Growing Up in the Black Belt*. New York: American Council on Education.

Jones, LeRoi, 1961, *Home Social Essays*. New York: Morrow.

Karmel, Marjorie, 1959, *Thank You, Dr. Lamaze*. New York: Doubleday.

Kochman, Thomas, 1970, "Toward an Ethnography of Black American Speech Behavior," in *Afro-American Anthropology: Contemporary Perspectives*, Norman E. Whitten, Jr. and John F. Szwed, eds., pp. 145–162. New York: Free Press.

Lang, Raven, 1972, *Birth Book*. Palo Alto, Calif.: Genesis Press.

Leacock, Eleanor B., 1969, *Teaching and Learning in City Schools: A Comparative Study*. New York: Basic Books.

Lewis, Hylan, 1955, *Blackways of Kent*. Chapel Hill: University of North Carolina Press.

Liebow, Elliot, 1967, *Tally's Corner: A Study of Negro Streetcorner Men*. Boston: Little, Brown.

Lomax, Alan, 1970, "The Homogeneity of African-Afro-American Musical Style," in *Afro-American Anthropology: Contemporary Perspectives*, Norman E. Whitten, Jr. and John F. Szwed, eds., pp. 181–201. New York: Free Press.

Malcolm X, 1964, *The Autobiography of Malcolm X*. New York: Grove.

Murphree, Alice H., 1969, "A Functional Analysis of Southern Folk Beliefs Concerning Birth, *American Journal of Obstetrics and Gynecology*, 102:125–134.

Myrdal, Gunnar, 1944, *An American Dilemma*. New York: Harper & Row.

Ogbu, John U., 1974, *The Next Generation: An Ethnography of Education in an Urban Neighborhood*. New York: Academic Press.

Powdermaker, Hortense, 1939, *After Freedom*. New York: Viking.

Rainwater, Lee and William L. Yancey, (eds.), 1967, *The Moynihan Report and the Politics of Controversy*. Cambridge, Mass.: M.I.T. Press.

Smith, Raymond T., 1956, *The Negro Family in British Guiana: Family Structure and Social Status in the Villages*. New York: Humanities Press.

Stack, Carol B., 1974, *All Our Kin: Strategies for Survival in a Black Community*. New York: Harper & Row.

Thompson, Ralph B. (ed.), 1975, *Florida Statistical Abstract*. Gainesville, Fla.: University of Florida Press.

Turner, Victor W., 1969, *The Ritual Process: Structure and Anti-Structure*. Chicago: Aldine.

U.S. Bureau of the Census, 1970, *Census of Population and Housing*. Machine Readable Data File. Count One.

————, 1970, *Census of Population and Housing*. Machine Readable Data File. Count Four.

Valentine, Charles A., 1968, *Culture and Poverty: Critique and Counter-Proposals*. Chicago: University of Chicago Press.

Van Gennep, Arnold, 1960, *The Rites of Passage*. Chicago: University of Chicago Press.

Warner, William Lloyd, 1962, *American Life: Dream or Reality*. Chicago: University of Chicago Press.

Wright, Richard, 1940, *Native Son*. New York: Harper & Row.

Young, Virginia H., 1970, "Family and Childhood in a Southern Negro Community," *American Anthropologist*, 72:269–288.

CASE STUDIES IN CONTEMPORARY AMERICAN CULTURE (NORTH AMERICA)

Aschenbrenner   Lifelines: Black Families in Chicago

Daner   The American Children of Krsna: A Study of the Hare Krsna Movement

Davidson   Chicano Prisoners: The Key to San Quentin

Friedland/Nelkin   Migrant: Agricultural Workers in America's Northeast

Hicka   Appalachian Valley

Hostetler/Huntington   Children in Amish Society: Socialization and Community Education (CSEC)

Hostetler/Huntington   The Hutterites of North America

Jacobs   Fun City: An Ethnographic Study of a Retirement Community

Keiser   The Vice Lords: Warriors of the Streets

Kunkel/Kennard   Spout Spring: A Black Community in the Ozarks

Madsen   Mexican Americans of South Texas, 2/E

O'Toole   Watts and Woodstock: Identity and Culture in the United States and South Africa

Partridge   The Hippie Ghetto: The Natural History of a Subculture

Pilcher   The Portland Longshoremen: A Dispersed Urban Community

Rosenfeld   "Shut Those Thick Lips!": A Study of Slum School Failure (CSEC)

Sugarman   Daytop Village: A Therapeutic Community

Ward   Them Children: A Study in Language Learning (CSEC)

Wolcott   The Man in the Principal's Office: An Ethnography (CSEC)